ORBS

AND THE

AFTERLIFE

SURVIVAL OF THE SOUL

Virginia M. Hummel

Hummel, Virginia M. – Orbs and the Afterlife: Survival of the Soul

Library of Congress No. 2015921323

ISBN 978-0-9834787-4-4 (trade paperback.)
ISBN 978-0-9834787-3-7 (eBook)

Cover Design: Virginia Hummel
Cover Photo: "Little boy and orb" © Virginia Hummel
Cover Photo: "Forest Orbs" © Monika Moehwald-Doelz
Interior Design: Virginia M. Hummel
Author Photo: Mark Davidson Photography

Due to a lack of quality control for the print on demand (POD) process, sometimes photos in this book may appear distorted or off color. Please visit OrbWhisperer.com/book-photos to view many of these photos online.

This book is dedicated to the Seekers and Believers

Contents

© Paul Mahal. Virginia Hummel with an orb.

"While I was seeking and searching mentally, psychically and occultly to discover 'the breakthrough' to Spirit for which I longed, the Light of the Unity of all things, all creatures, all Beings, all Hosts, all Powers dwelt within me in ineffable glory. 'I am the Light of the World,' means just that."

~ Helen Greaves

INTRODUCTION

This book contains a decade of my research, photos and experiences with the orb phenomenon. Within these pages are stories and photographs from around the world of others who have also experienced this curious phenomenon. You will have the opportunity to view photographs and read firsthand accounts of those who have interacted with what might be the tunnel through which we travel to Heaven. Most importantly, this book will offer you the opportunity to discover how the orb phenomenon is connected to human consciousness and our roles as eternal beings.

My journey began on February 4, 2006, when I received a telephone call that my beautiful son Christopher, age twenty-five, had been killed in an accident. Immediately, I began to experience after-death communication followed by the appearance of a brilliant ball of light or orb twenty months after the death of my son. From there it led to people, places, research and ongoing experiences with orbs and the consciousness behind them. It was this visual connection to the spiritual realm that brought me great comfort, helped to shift my perception of death and heal my grief.

It is through the orb phenomenon and other Spiritually Transformative Experiences (STEs) that we can receive healing and validation that we survive death and that a connection with our loved ones is possible once they have crossed over to the other side. We can use that knowledge and experience to help alleviate the pain caused by loss and the illusion of separation and begin to proactively comfort and heal ourselves.

We hope you will explore the pages and photos contained within this book with an open mind and heart and then pick up your camera and experience the orb phenomenon for yourself. Only then may you truly understand the joy, excitement and healing that can come from experiencing the orb phenomenon first hand.

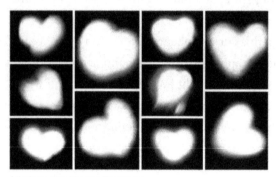

All photos © Naomi Fugiwara

CHAPTER ONE

"All truths are easy to understand once they are discovered;
the point is to discover them."

~ Galileo

Are Orbs Real?

As a child, I remember the utter amazement I felt each week as I sat riveted to the television set watching "The Undersea World of Jacques Cousteau."[1] His 1968-1974 television series introduced the world to the incomparable beauty of sea life. With great excitement, I learned that our oceans teamed with all sorts of colorful, unique-looking creatures. Without Cousteau's passion for exploration and his camera, I may never have known about these amazing life forms. How was it possible that these creatures lived virtually next door, yet I was wholly unaware of their presence?

In 1972, I was mesmerized by Apollo 17's image of the iconic blue marble that was Earth; one of the most significant photos of the twentieth-century. Awed by the planet's beauty and grace and overwhelmed by the vastness of her size, I was also touched by her fragility. She was a beautiful blue orb floating in an infinite sea of darkness, in a universe without end.

It was beyond the scope of my imagination to grasp what I had seen. This is where I lived. The photograph compelled me to wonder what else might be out there. What other significant discoveries have yet to be made? What other photographs might change our world as we know it?

God has filled our universe with such a large variety of life forms. In the macrocosm of space are still undiscovered galaxies, stars and life beyond our wildest imagining. Likewise, in the microcosm of quantum physics we have now discovered quarks, which are basic building blocks of matter. Between these two realms lie infinite possibilities.

Photo 1 © Patricia Alexander. Virginia with an orb at her fingertips after requesting one to appear.

The truth is revealed for each of us on many different occasions and in many different forms. It is always there waiting to be discovered. Columbus, Galileo and Sir Isaac Newton stood at the forefront of history's significant discoveries. Their willingness to open their minds, follow their passion and explore the unknown, forged a pathway for others to follow—and follow they did.

Once again, we stand at a crossroads. We have recently discovered a new frontier; ready to be explored and embraced by those who are courageous enough to embark on the mission. Little does it matter that it is currently scoffed at by skeptics. This doesn't make it less real, and for the explorer it raises the stakes and heightens the challenge.

Orbs have been identified in photographs as spheres of light as far back as 1907 where M. Bessy captured a large orb floating through the botanical gardens in Basle, Switzerland. The arrival of digital cameras allowed us to capture orbs with ease yet skeptics believed the "orbs" were all nothing but lens flare, moisture or dust particles. We have discovered, however, that along with the lens flare, dust or moisture was something else. Many of these particles were actual forms or embodiments.

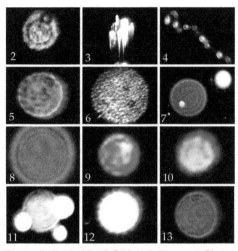

Photos 2, 5, 10, 12, 13 © Virginia Hummel. Photos 3, 7 © Monika Moehwald-Doelz. Photos 4, 6, 11 © Naomi Fugiwara. Photo 8 © Marcus Lang. Photo 9 © Carol Danforth.

Manifesting in a variety of colors and sizes, orbs can appear with concentric circles, coronas, mandalas, bumps, knobs and tracks. They can be pale or wispy, brilliant white or colored, and can reveal a multitude of interior designs. They may also appear as a tube or streak of light, depending on the speed of the camera shutter.

Other descriptions of orbs include disk shapes, small flashes of light, squiggly snake-like oddities, light spheres in geometric formation, and glittering arrays of plasma clouds. Websites and social media pages display breathtaking photos along with discussion forums for devoted orb fans where they can compare notes and share their insights as well as their passion for these benevolent beings of light or *orbs*.

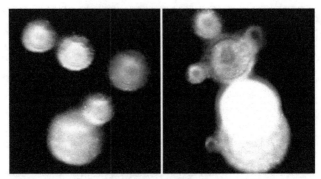

Photo 14 (left), 15 (right). Multicolored orbs in geometric formation. © Naomi Fugiwara.

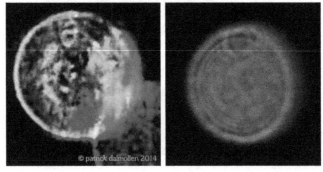

Photo 16 (left) © Patrick Dalmollen. Photo 17 (right) © Virginia Hummel. Faces inside orbs.

Each orb photograph is an original masterpiece, whether it is of a pale wispy sphere or a brilliant ball of streaking light. Animals, mandalas and spirals, along with letters and numbers have also been discovered in orbs. One of the most intriguing aspects of orbs is the discovery of human faces inside them.

Orb photographs demand that we question the very nature of our existence. Does consciousness survive death? Could orbs be a physical manifestation of human consciousness? Does the presence of orbs affirm that we are truly eternal beings?

Over the past ten years, I've been driven by my burning desire to know if these beautiful forms are in some way connected to my son Christopher who died in 2006. I've taken tens of thousands of photos, captured many hours of iPhone and infrared videos, and researched, experimented with and experienced this phenomenon. One thought has remained at the forefront of my mind, unyielding and immutable: *an orb can be a physical manifestation of a soul or consciousness energy.*

What would it mean to millions of parents who have lost their children to know that their child lives on? What kind of comfort and peace might it bring to those who are grieving to be able to photograph the essence of their loved one near them? If evidence existed linking orbs to our loved ones, I would do everything in my power to find it, and I knew my son Christopher would help me with the task.

Photo 18. Streaking orb. © Monika Moehwald-Doelz.

For a large number of people living on this planet, orbs have become a very real occurrence. My own discoveries regarding orbs have led me to consider them a beacon of hope that we are not alone in this vast universe.

Those of you who are new to the phenomenon of orbs, may I suggest that you read *The Orb Project* for an in-depth look at orbs from a scientific perspective. I also found this book interesting because authors, Míċeál Ledwith, a theologian, viewed the orb phenomenon from a scientific perspective, while Klaus Heinemann, a physicist, focused on a spiritual perspective.

The following information is derived from my personal experiences with orbs as well as information gathered from different sources during my research. I am constantly surprised and delighted to receive new information via emails newly published stories of near-death experiences (NDE), and firsthand experiences.

Dust or Moisture

Many people contend that orbs are nothing more than dust particles in the air; depending on the picture, that may be true. However, according to Mícéal Ledwith, D.D., LL.D., co-author of *The Orb Project*, "A careful analysis of the data collected in this study clearly shows that the orb phenomenon is real and cannot be explained away by the myriad suggestions that have been produced to account for it, such as raindrops or fog, dust particles or pollen in the air, lens flare, bokeh [blurs], or digital processing errors."[2] Orbs have even been photographed in Class 7 clean rooms used in research laboratories where airborne particles above a certain size may affect research or quality control.[3]

It is easy to confuse real orbs with dust, moisture and lens flare. I was also skeptical about orbs captured on camera. However, I had the good fortune to experience orbs first-hand without the aid of a camera, so I know they do exist. The trick is to figure out which is which in our photos, as I've also seen lens flare that looks strikingly similar to some orbs. A conscientious orb photographer will photograph dust, moisture and lens flare just to learn the difference between false orbs and real orbs.

Some skeptics argue that orbs in photos are actually dust particles. The basis for this argument is that orb photos are really reflections from dust particles, illuminated by the flash and taken within inches of the lens.

In Photos 19 and 20 below, we see a few orbs and what appears to be a moving or streaking orb. After taking the photos, I noticed that the "streaking orb" was in the same spot in each photo. I checked my lens and discovered a hair which had caused the effect. It is important to question the validity of your orb photos and rule out dust, moisture and in this case a hair on the lens. Photo 21 shows a streaking orb and an orb. Photo 22 shows real orbs and a hair on the lens which looks like a streaking orb.

Since we usually see the entirety of the orb in a picture and rarely see an orb behind another object, skeptics reason they must be dust or moisture particles captured close to the lens. Sometimes even a hair or water spot on the lens can be confused with an orb.

Photo 19 (left), Photo 20 (right) © Virginia Hummel. A few orbs shown with a hair on the lens.

Photo 21 (left). Streaking orb with orbs. Photo 22 (right). Hair on lens with real orbs. © Virginia Hummel

People often wonder why we don't see more photos of orbs partially obscured by an object. This has been a nagging question for orb enthusiasts and skeptics alike. I could reason that since they appear to possess a consciousness, they are choosing to materialize in front of objects in order to be photographed.

According to Klaus Heinemann, Ph.D., co-author of *The Orb Project,* "Dust particles or droplets must be within a few inches from the camera lens to cause 'fake' orb-like images."[4]

Monika Moehwald-Doelz worked for a large U.S. photographic company for many years. She now lives in Germany with her husband. After she left the company, she began to take pictures, concentrating specifically on orbs. She photographs orbs nearly every day using several cameras. Many of her photographs are excellent examples of the orb phenomenon and appear throughout the book and my website.[5]

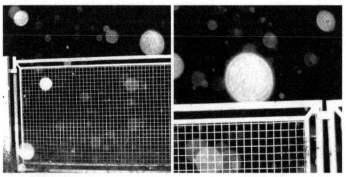

Photo 23 (left). Orbs appear in front of and behind a gate. Photo 24 (right). Color contrasted orb behind gate. © Monika Moehwald-Doelz.

One evening, Monika captured a photograph that shows orbs behind a gate and far enough from the lens to be impossible to identify as dust or moisture particles. (Photo 23)

The photo was then color contrasted. If the large orb in the upper right of the photo were in front of the gate, we would see a color variation on the top rail. (Photo 24) The photo also allows us to see three very bright orbs that appear in the foreground and in front of the gate along with many orbs that appear beyond the gate and fence in the background.

The following photos show some moving or streaking orbs. In Photo 25 we see a streaking orb upper left along with several orbs that look as if some pieces are missing. The miniscule "orbs" are actually rain drops.

Photo 26 shows a group of streaking orbs where each orb was composed of several smaller orbs. According to Klaus Heinemann, Ph.D., co-author of *The Orb Project*, orbs have been clocked at five hundred mph.

Slower moving orbs have also been captured. Photos 31 and 32 were taken by two different people yet the photos seem to suggest a similar movement from these larger orbs.

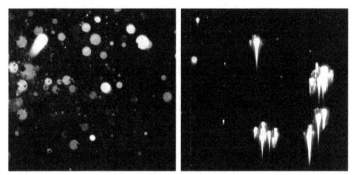

Photo 25 (left) © Lucy Lewis. Streaking orb upper left, normal orbs and miniscule orb like rain drops. Photo 26 (right). Streaking orbs. © Monika Moehwald-Doelz.

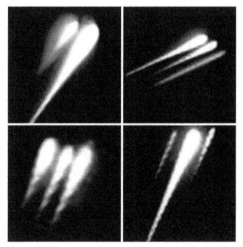

Photo 27 (lower left), Photo 28 (upper left), Photo 29 (upper right), Photo 30 (lower left) © Naomi Fugiwara Streaking orbs.

Naomi Fugiwara takes the majority of her orb photographs facing the angel's wings on her door which you can partially see in Photo 31. She seems to capture all colors and sizes of orbs. I also capture the majority of my orb photos facing the same area in my room.

Photo 31 (left) © Naomi Fugiwara. Photo 32 (right) © Virginia Hummel. Slow moving orbs.

Lens Flare

Lens flare is the blight of orb photographers. We can create lens flare when we shoot into a light source such as the sun, moon, landscape or indoor lighting. Reflections of the camera flash from mirrors or windows can also cause lens flare. I cannot tell you how disappointed I am to see an amazing photo only to realize upon closer inspection that lens flare had caused the "orb" or "energy being."

Lens flare can manifest as colored rings, circles, starbursts, discs, "energy beings" and sometimes faces, depending on the camera manufacturer. They may be in a row across the image, but typically, they spread widely across the scene. They can be a series of colored "orbs" or a mixture of discs, blocks, tapered cones and rainbow colors. The location can change with the camera's movement in relation to light sources. The shape of the aperture also affects the formation of anomalies in the photographs. Photo 33 was taken into the sun and created a large flare that covered the palm tree. The upper left Photo 34 is a combination of colored discs and circles which are also common in lens flare photos. Photo 36 was also created by shooting into the sun. It looks as if there is a purple tornado and alien face. I saturated the colors that were already there to make it easy to observe.

Photo 33 (lower left), Photo 34 (upper left), Photo 35 (lower right) © Virginia Hummel. Photo 36 (upper right) © Brenda Layton. All photos lens flare.

Photo 37 (lower left) © Virginia Hummel. Glass table reflection. Photo 38 (upper left) © Cha Cha. Red and green lens flare. Photo 39 (upper right) © Marja. Orange lens flare. Photo 40 (lower right) © Joyce Lindsay. Blue green lens flare.

Above the flare that looks like a head and face in Photo 36 we see a reddish disk shape with a white dot which is a very common in false orb photos. The whitish blue or greenish dots we see in photos taken into a light source are most often mistaken for orbs and can be seen in Photo 40. They are lens flare created by the mirrors and aperture of the camera.

Different camera manufacturers create different kinds of lens flare but they all can be recreated. Grab your camera and shoot into the sun and other light sources to create lens flare so you will know the specific types of lens flare your camera creates. This way it will be easier for you to distinguish real orbs from false orbs.

Photo 37, lower left, shows a common type of occurrence that is caused by a reflection off a window or through glass. This one was caused from my glass patio table. Photo 38 is also a common lens flare created when shooting into the sun and can create reddish "false orbs" along with the green face as is the orange "orb like" ball in Photo 39 and the blue green "orb" in Photo 40.

Photo 41 © Virginia Hummel. Lens flare.

These types of photos are exciting and fun and stimulate our imagination, but they are *not* "orbs or "energy beings." They are lens flare. The important thing about these photos, regardless of whether or not they are real, is that they encourage us think of spirit and the connection available to us.

Orb photographers also struggle with camera movement which can accidently create orb or paranormal looking photos but in reality, are just photographer error.

Camera Movement

The following photos are created by camera movement. As we depress the button to capture a photo, we can inadvertently move the camera and the "orb" appears as a continuous streak of light. Photo 42 was taken during a memorial service. It appears as if angels have arrived and are standing by.

Photo 42 (top) © Michal Curry. Camera movement.
Photo 43 (lower left), Photo 44 (middle), Photo 45
(lower right) © Virginia Hummel. All photos are
camera movement.

Personally, it is quite a moving photo. Who wouldn't want to see angels near their loved one? But as I studied this photo and the odd but identical "J" squiggly lights, I realized that camera movement and an auto delayed aperture setting for night time caused this "angel entities" photo.

To prove my point, I took several photos of landscape lights at night and deliberately made a "J" movement with my camera as I depressed the button to mimic the "J" in the angel photo. It was possible to create virtually any letter. (See Photos 43, 44, 45)

Notice the similarities with the angels in Photo 42 and Photo 43. The delayed aperture setting and camera movement created a double exposure with the people and the palm trees. The "J" hooks of light are also similar. I see so many interesting photos that look magical but turn out to be camera movement.

It doesn't dispel my belief in spirit or my ability to capture spirit on camera. Instead, it becomes much more important to question each photo to be certain of what we are seeing. If we rule out dust, moisture, lens flare and camera movement, what do we have left that might explain the orb phenomenon?

CHAPTER TWO

"There is a crack in everything. That's how the light gets in."
~ Leonard Cohen

What Are Orbs?

Current research suggests two theories about the physical properties of orbs. The first theory is that orbs are subtle energy. MIT and Princeton educated physicist, Claude Swanson, Ph.D., author of *The Synchronized Universe Series,* says, "Subtle energy is a confusing subject for the Western scientist...it responds to and interacts with thought, making it unlike any known force."[6]

Subtle Energy

During the filming of my grief documentary, I asked Dr. Swanson why he thought the phenomenon of orbs was important to the scientific community. He said, "Orbs are important because they behave as if it's a different form of energy, it's not a form of energy that our science understands. It's not electromagnetic, it's not gravitational, and it's not nuclear. It is some other form of energy that we don't have a theory for in Western science and yet we have very good documentation that it really occurs."

In Volume II of *The Synchronized Universe*, Swanson writes:

> Subtle energy is called by many names including Chi, Qi, Prana, OD, Orgone, Time Density, Bioplasma, Mana, Life Force, etc. It is the bridge between current physics and many anomalous effects observed in the laboratory, but which violate current science. The presence of subtle energy is believed to modify current physical law introducing a variety of phenomena related to consciousness and paranormal phenomena."[7]

Orbs have been detected on photographic film, by electromagnetic sensors, by cameras, and other means. They illustrate the possibility that subtle energy, because it is a non-linear field, can become concentrated to an extent that it becomes self-stabilizing. It does not require matter in order for it to exist.[8]

Photo 46 © Virginia Hummel. Daytime orb.

Suzanne

In 2012, I had the opportunity to discuss the orb phenomenon with Suzanne Giesemann. Suzanne is a retired U.S. Navy Commander. She served as special assistant to the Chief of Naval Operations and as aide to the Chairman of the Joint Chiefs of Staff on 9/11.[9] Today she is the author of ten books, a spiritual teacher, and an evidential medium. Dr. Wayne Dyer says, "Suzanne is an exceptionally gifted visionary."[10]

After years of meditation, she began to have her own intuitive experiences. She connects with higher consciousness through a channel called Sanaya. "Sanaya has told us that she is a collective consciousness of minds with both a feminine and masculine energy. This energy comes from a higher dimension than our own. When I bring through Sanaya's words, I am "tapping in" to higher consciousness."

Suzanne knew very little about the phenomenon of orbs and as I began to ask her questions, Sanaya came through with answers from a higher dimension. When asked what orbs were made of Sanaya answered:

> What is consciousness made of? What is the electromagnetic spectrum made of? It is pure energy, a subtle energy. You call it prana. It is the life force energy only using the available light sources.

> An orb is evidence of life. It carries the energy of life itself. You will see far more orbs around trees and other life forms as their energy adds to the life forms. Orbs are sentient beings if you wish to call them beings, coalescing energy that can form and dissolve at will for your enjoyment and for the lessons placed there by higher consciousness. But they are fully conscious and sentient themselves. How do you like that? Like the cells in your body, your cells are all conscious. They are orderly and have their own system.

> Within the orb, there is a hierarchy and a greater guiding consciousness, and you can communicate with this consciousness at will, of course. All consciousness is one, and you really only need to communicate telepathically.

> There is no need to speak aloud, although if you can add emotion to your words and invite in this consciousness we

will quite enjoy playing with you and giving you a show. If you want colors, ask for them. It is indeed true that the colors represent the higher movement along the spectrum, but do not discount the sacredness of those that merely play white.[11]

The following photo was taken as I called in the orbs to play with me. There is one sitting in the palm of my left hand, albeit a very faint one. My research and experience tells me there is a greater consciousness at work. Whether it is a subtle energy or one of plasma I cannot say for sure. I only know the pure joy I feel from interacting with them.

Photo 47 © Patricia Alexander. Virginia Hummel with orbs.

Conscious Communication

One night I was awakened out of a deep sleep by the strong urging to go outside and take orb photos. I was irritated that "they", whoever "they" were, were insisting that I get out of my warm bed and go outside in the cold and dark and take orbs photos. It was 3AM. I silently argued with this force for fifteen minutes before I grudgingly grabbed my coat and camera and headed outside.

After taking maybe twenty or thirty photos, I came back inside to check them. Tired and cranky, I started to hit the delete button when I noticed something very unusual. Of the tens of thousands of photos I have taken, and the thousands of orb photos I have seen on the internet, I have never seen this.

From behind my Jacuzzi, heading upward at a slight angle appeared to be a red orb with a white plasma ring that reminded me of something out of Star Trek. There are several other normal orbs in Photo 48. Photo 49 showed the same orb straight on. Photo 50 is an enlargement of the original.

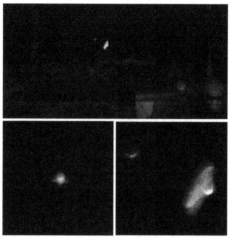

Photo 48 (top). Orb with plasma field. Photo 49 (lower left). Front view of orb. Photo 50 (lower right). Enlargement of Photo 48. © Virginia Hummel.

The timing of this experience cannot be coincidental nor can the fact I was purposely awakened and strongly urged to go outside in the middle of the night to take orbs photos. Once again, my research and experience shows me that there is a greater consciousness at work in this universe and that consciousness is somehow connected with the orb phenomenon. In my search to discover others who may have had a similar type of experience, I came across John and Katie's story.

John and Katie

Katie Hall and John Pickering, co-authors of *Beyond Photography: Encounters with orbs, angels and mysterious light –forms!* share an interesting story regarding orbs and consciousness. They had been outside shooting orb photos and watching the night sky. They could view several constellations including Canis Major from their vantage point. They both saw a brighter light that came out of nowhere and hung above the tree tops before moving off out of their view of Canis Major and disappearing into the night sky which John identified as a UFO.

John has had long interest in astronomy and was familiar with the various constellations. He also knew it wasn't a satellite or airplane. The following morning, they reviewed their photos and discovered a grouping of orbs in one particular photo that didn't appear to be random. (See Photo 52) It was taken of Katie at ground level. They pulled out some star charts and discovered the configuration of the orbs matched eleven of the twenty-one stars in Canis Major.[12]

Photo 51 (left), Photo 52 (right) © 'Beyond Photography: Encounters with orbs, angels and mysterious light forms!' by Katie Hall & John Pickering, published by John Hunt Publishing Ltd. 2006. Reproduced with permission from John Hunt Publishing Ltd. Orbs that formed the same configuration as Canis Major.

If the orbs captured in their photo were merely dust, how is it possible that "dust" could form an exact replica of a constellation and be captured on camera at the very moment both Katie and John witness the brilliant light appear in the night sky near Canis Major? In my professional opinion, this was no coincidence.

The colored orbs in Photo 53 also give me the same feeling Katie and John had about their photograph. Notice that there are several orbs that stand out to form a pattern. I have yet to sit down and try to align them with a star chart but something tells me there is a message in that photo.

My research and experience tell me a higher consciousness was at work here. Both Katie and John seem to agree. Claude Swanson, Ph.D. states, "Subtle energy is called by many names including Chi, Qi, Prana, OD, Orgone, Time Density, Bioplasma, Mana and Life Force." Is this Life Force or subtle energy also conscious energy?

Photo 53 © Virginia Hummel. Orbs that stand out and appear to form a pattern.

Plasma Energy

The second theory regarding the physical property of an orb is that it consists of plasma. Plasma is the most common form of matter. It is an ionized gas with electrical properties that create a magnetic field.

Klaus Heinemann earned his Ph.D. in experimental physics. He has worked in materials science research at NASA and University of California Los Angeles, and as a research professor at Stanford University. Heinemann says:

> It would have to be expected that it [an orb] is some sort of "energetic globe of plasma," which would also explain why

orbs typically show up as circular images…an orb is a physical manifestation…that can be detected as light, i.e. as electromagnetic waves in the visible spectral range.[13]

Míceál Ledwith, D.D., LL.D., co-author of *The Orb Project* has data to show that orbs can manipulate the electromagnetic charges recorded by the camera. He suggests that using an ionizing meter can corroborate the presence of orbs, as their appearance seems to accompany a change in ionization.

Ledwith states that orbs are easier to capture when there is rain or high humidity. Although one must be diligent not to identify raindrops as orbs. Ledwith also believes orbs react to the photon energy emitted by the flash, which excites the molecules inside the orb. The orbs then expel low wave infrared light, which is captured on your camera. Photo 54 shows three orbs in fluorescence.

Photo 54 (left) © Linda Strausbaugh. Three orbs in full fluorescence. Photo 55 (right) © Monika Moehwald-Doelz. Light emitted from the orbs were affected by the shape of the camera's shutter.

He also says, "If a process of fluorescence aided by the attraction of free electrons through ionization is what enables the orbs to be photographed, then the orbs must *be electromagnetic* in nature, and *most likely are energy fields of some kind.*"[14]

While photographing orbs, Ledwith noticed they began to take the shape of the shutter leaves on his camera. He knew that objects scatter, reflect, or absorb light, which didn't account for the strange shapes appearing in his photos. He realized that orbs were creating their own light source, possible through the process of fluorescence.

I have captured orbs in various shapes depending on the manufacturer of my camera. My Sony NEX 3 sometimes creates an oval effect to an orb while my two Nikon Coolpix cameras can create a rounded edge and rectangle image. Photo 55 was taken by Monika Moehwald-Doelz. The aperture on her camera seemed to affect the light emitted by the orbs as they were captured in this photo.

A gentleman named Tim contacted me through my website with a description of an orb he saw one night that was not round but hexagonal in shape. He writes:

> I just happened to see one orb with my naked eye. Even though it was not captured with a camera, it was still hexagonal in shape but tubular as well. It was purple, green, pink, and blue. It was very early in the morning, there was no light in the room and the windows were blacked out. I had to watch it very closely to believe what I was seeing. The orb was hex shaped and tubular the entire time, and stayed the same size, shape, and colors as it flew. It almost looked as if you could put a hex wrench over it.

> It came out of one wall and flew over my bed and went into the other wall. Not a straight line, rather kind of slow and curving as it flew. I didn't have a camera but I know what I saw. I have watched that same area and taken pictures at different times and have not seen anymore.

Ledwith also refers to another type of occurrence called *plasmoid clouds* not attributed to camera malfunction and appear as white or colored veils. colored veils. Photos 56 and 57 are examples of Ledwith's plasmoid clouds or veils. Photo 56 also has a bright streaking orb, upper right corner, and a wide semicircle lens flare above it. Photo 57 has several streaking orbs along with the red veil.

Photo 56 (left). Gold plasma veil with a streaking orb and various other orbs. Photo 57 (right). Red plasma veil and several streaking orbs. © Diana Davatgar.

We also photograph plasma manifesting in different shapes that appear too coincidental to be just be random clouds or mists. These shapes lend validity to the theory of subtle energy and the presence of consciousness.

Could Photo 58 demonstrate a combination of consciousness and an example of a plasmoid field Ledwith spoke of earlier? It appears to have the profile of a human face. What do you see? Could the letter 'S' be just a coincidence in Photo 59 or a deliberate attempt to communicate? Are the animal shapes in Photo 60 and 61 a camera malfunction or an example of plasma, subtle energy and/or consciousness?

Photo 62 and 63 were taken by Patrick Dalmollen who used Instrumental Trans-Dimensional Communication via Ultrasonic Air Humidifier Method to obtain these remarkable photos. Photos are taken as the humidifier releases steam.

Captured inside the steam are these images. Can you see the human like images revealed inside them? Are these coincidences or a manifestation of subtle energy and consciousness? Are loved ones and others who have crossed over trying to communicate with us?

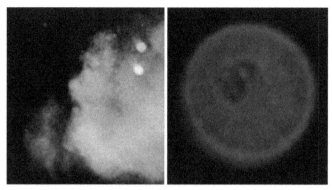

Photo 58 (left) © Wendy Byrd. A face appears in the plasma cloud.
Photo 59 (right) © Patricia Alexander. A letter appears inside of an orb.

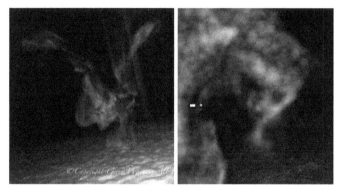

Photo 60 (left), 61(right) © Gerry Warner. Animal shapes appears in plasma clouds.

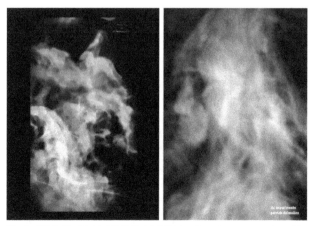

Photo 62 (left), 63 (right) © Patrick Dalmollen. Images captured by Air Humidifier Method. https://www.facebook.com/Lightworker1978

John

Heinemann's description of an orb as an "energetic globe of plasma" reminded me of several stories about orbs and their descriptions. In *Beyond Photography, Encounters with Orbs, Angels and Mysterious Light-Forms*, co-author John Pickering's experience as a young boy caught my attention, as did his description of ball lightning, which is associated with plasma. John writes:

> When thunder rolled and the summer storm walked on legs of lightning across the land, my grandmother would always take precautions. She would draw the curtains, cover all the mirrors with tea towels and open the back door. She always left the back door open to let out a thunderbolt in case one came down the chimney.
>
> Where she got this custom I don't know, but it was meant to protect the house against lightning and thunderbolts. Nowadays this may sound a rather silly and superstitious thing to have done, but like much folklore and superstition, it was founded on fact.
>
> To a boy of nine, thunderbolts sounded both exciting and frightening, though I had no idea what a thunderbolt actually was. Not until I saw one. It was August and my grandmother and I were sheltering in the backroom as the electrical storm boomed and flashed over the valley. She had taken all her precautions and the interior of the house was dim behind the drawn curtains.
>
> Suddenly in the darkened room, there was an intense glow of light. Right by the front of the fireplace, just as though it had come down the chimney, was a ball of shimmering blue light. I remember it being the size of a football, perhaps a little larger. Floating a foot or so off the floor it seemed to ripple, like something seen though a summer heat haze. The luminous sphere seemed to be wobbling slightly as it glided slowly towards the settee.

My grandmother quickly grabbed me and pulled me to the other side of the room. Wide eyed we watched it from behind the big polished oak table. I can recall an acrid smell and the air seemed to tingle. I remember feeling that prickling sensation known as "pins and needles" dancing all over my skin.

The ball of bluish light had drifted around the settee, stopping for a few moments in front of the glass china cabinet, just as though looking at its own reflection. I watched it half in fear; half in fascination. Moments later, it glided through the doorway and into the kitchen. Extricating myself from my grandmother's grip, I cautiously followed just in time to see it exit the house through the back door.

Running outside I looked vainly around, but the ball of light had disappeared; apparently swallowed up by the storm that had brought it! For whatever reasons my grandmother's precautions had worked; the thunderbolt had obligingly left the house through the open back door. It was an amazing experience, one of those magical childhood memories that have stayed with me over the years, but yet I've never seen ball lightening again.[15]

Was John's "ball lightning" similar to Klaus Heinemann's plasma globes or was it something else, perhaps a combination of both plasma and subtle energy? It appeared to exhibit a consciousness when it stopped and looked at itself in the reflection of the china cabinet before it deliberately made its way through the kitchen and out the door. This description matches another published story of an orb that also appears to have characteristics similar to plasma, yet exhibits consciousness similar to subtle energy.

Vladimir

Vladimir Megre is the author of *The Ringing Cedars of Russia Series,* a set of nine non-fiction works that has sold over ten million copies and translated into twenty languages. "The series of nine books tells of a remarkable woman named Anastasia, discovered in 1995 by Vladimir Megre, a Siberian trader. He spent three days with her, during which she displayed such astounding knowledge, power and wisdom that he abandoned his business and at her request began to write this series...The purity and power of her words is provoking an outpouring of joy and hope in people from all walks of life."[16]

In book two, Megre recounts a story told by Anastasia's grandfather as he watched her as a toddler alone in a glade.

> We looked up and saw it. Over the meadow, we saw hanging a small spherical mass, pulsating and glowing with a pale blue light. We could see a whole multitude of fiery discharges inside its transparent covering, giving the effect of multicolored lightning. We could feel some kind of unknown and unseen power in it. But there was no sense of fear in this power...it seemed to be radiating a pleasant, languid grace.[17]

This sphere appeared to protect and help little Anastasia. She could raise her open arms and summon it into her embrace. It lay with her as she fell asleep.

> It was capable of changing form into a mist-like bluish glow with more power than the Sun's rays...expanding and dissolving into space...the sphere would momentarily disappear then reappear, as though it were somehow excited."[18] Anastasia would communicate with the blue orb and it continued to protect her into adulthood. When asked what she called it, she answered, "Good.[19]

After reading these stories, I wondered if the ball of lightning that John saw as a child was an orb that manifested with the help of the electrical charge from a storm. Spirit seems to gravitate to electronic equipment, such as the TV, radio, lights, computers, and cell phones, in addition to recordings like EVP (electronic voice phenomenon) as a means of communication.

There have been many unusual experiences when the lights blinked and I then felt the presence of my son or Spirit; or I would get a sense of my son's presence in my car and suddenly our song would play on the radio. Several times, he has used my computer as well as his cell phone to communicate his presence.

Photo 64 © Nancy Myers. A moving orb in a V shape.

Could this ability to manipulate electricity mean that orbs are electromagnetic in nature, or could orbs be subtle energy with the ability to manipulate electromagnetic fields? Are they a combination of both or something completely different? Photo 64 shows the letter "V" created by an orb. Is it coincidence or perhaps a message? In several orb videos, I have seen them flash and change colors much like a plasma globe found in a lab.

Although science has yet to conclude whether or not orbs are plasma, subtle energy, or a combination of both, one factor is certain: both sides seem to agree that the orb phenomenon is real.

We know several things to be true about the orb phenomenon.

1. Orbs can physically manifest in a circular form as well as a cloud, mist or "plasmoid veils."
2. Orbs can be photographed and seen with the naked eye.
3. Orbs appear to fluoresce.
4. Orbs can be detected as light i.e. as electromagnetic waves in the visible spectral range.
5. Orbs appear in a multitude of colors coinciding with the visible and invisible light spectrum.
6. Orbs can affect a Gauss Meter which measures the level of magnetic field emitted by all common electrical appliances and equipment.
7. According to firsthand accounts of physical touch with an orb there appears to be an absence of heat or cold. (See Ashlee's story in Chapter Three, Diandra's Story in Chapter Eleven and Dude! You're in My Face in Chapter Eleven.)
8. Orbs appear to react to thought or intention much the way subtle energy does.
9. Orbs appear in meaningful places and at meaningful times.
10. Orbs can respond to direct requests.

Many of us have had the opportunity to photograph orbs and even see them with our eyes without the aid of a camera. My first experience with the orb phenomenon arrived twenty months after the death of my son Christopher in the fall of 2007.

CHAPTER THREE

"The real voyage of discovery consists not in seeking new landscapes but in having new eyes."

~ Marcel Proust

The Light Being

Late one night I awoke shivering. A chill had descended in the high desert of Southern California where I lived. I slipped from my bed to turn off the air conditioner and as I stepped back into my darkened bedroom, I froze. A brilliant ball of white light, slightly larger than a ping-pong ball, was hovering before me in mid-air.

The light also seemed startled. After a momentary hesitation, it darted to my left, parallel to the wall in front of me, took a sharp left and followed that wall for about five feet before it disappeared. It left a trail of light much like a twirling Fourth of July sparkler.

My mind raced. Was there a burglar with a flashlight outside my sliding door? I bolted and ran through the house to check the locks. After I rechecked my alarm system, I rushed to my young daughter's bedside. She was sleeping soundly and I cautiously crept back to my bed; my senses hyper-alert.

Terrified, I drew the cold covers to my chin, shivering now for a different reason. I lay there wide-eyed in the dark, my heart still pounding as I listened for the slightest sound that could indicate an intruder. I tried to find a logical explanation for what I'd seen but could find none and my mind filled with frightening scenarios.

After I'd calmed down and was able to reason with myself, I realized the burglar scenario didn't ring true. There are blackout curtains on my windows and the light had started on a solid wall next to the sliding door. It would be impossible for a simple flashlight to penetrate the wall and create the bright white ball of light I'd seen hovering approximately three feet down from the ceiling and three feet out from the wall.

Photo 65 © Virginia Hummel. An orb similar to the one I saw in the middle of the night.

Then I considered something of a different nature. Could the ball of light have been a spiritual event: a light from God? Was it a new kind of ADC or after-death communication? Was it an angel, or better yet, did it have something to do with my son Chris who had been killed in a motorcycle accident twenty months earlier.

The following morning, I called a girlfriend and described what I'd witnessed the night before.

She simply said, "That was a light being."

"What's that?"

"A light being can be any number of things," she answered, "including an emanation from Spirit, an inter-dimensional being, our guides and angels, an extraterrestrial, or a sentient being. Who really knows for sure? But they are here to help us."

She told me that the International Orb and Light Being Conference scheduled at the Palm Springs Convention Center, was just a few weeks away.

"Are you kidding me?" I asked as I rolled my eyes. "An orb convention?"

The word "orb" is generally used to describe a ball of light seen in digital photos. They can appear as a sphere of light, circle of light, oval of light, ball of light, disc of light, and being of light. They have also been referred to in the near-death experiences as "globular or egg-shaped spheres of some sort."[20] I knew what an orb was but I hadn't heard the term "light being."

Orbs appeared in my photographs off and on for several years, but this was the first time I had seen one with my eyes. As I pondered the identity and meaning of "light being," I wondered again if it had anything to do with my son. I was a grieving parent. Was I onto valuable information, or just grasping for anything to make sense of my painful loss?

If I saw this "light being" with my eyes, there must be a reason. Through the years, I've learned that nothing is a coincidence. Carl Jung coined the term "synchronicity." He used it to describe the moment when the external and internal events of a person's mind seem to coincide perfectly. I believe it also describes the moment we recognize that we are divinely guided and led.

The skeptical side of me whispered that orbs in my photos were just dust or lens flare—but now I had experienced an orb first-hand. I thought orbs were an interesting phenomenon over the years, but not compelling enough to research, or spend any amount of time contemplating what they were.

After all, even if they were real, what possible meaning did they have in my life? How could they help me in my day-to-day living, with my relationships, my bills, or my job?

Photo 66 © Virginia Hummel. A single bright orb in my kitchen.

Yet now inner guidance or intuition was urging me to look into this phenomenon further. Was there a connection, a reason the ball of light had appeared that night, and was it important? I considered the event I had experienced in my bedroom as my personal invitation to attend the Palm Springs Conference to learn more about orbs.

Meanwhile, I discovered a few recent photos that contained orbs, taken after my son's accident when Logan, his five-year-old son, and his mother came to visit. I immediately began my research on orbs and light beings on the Internet.

There were only a handful of books on the subject at the time with varying opinions. One book, *The Orb Project*, by Míċeál Ledwith, D.D., LL.D. and Klaus Heinemann, Ph.D., provided some scientific insight into this relatively new field.[21]

A skeptic at heart, I knew the only way I would be able to learn exactly what orbs represented was to experience them for myself. I have always believed in life after death and that we are guided by Spirit if we are awake enough to recognize the signs. Yet, I didn't want to get my hopes up that orbs could in some way be connected to my son. But what if they were connected?

A memory came to mind and I recalled my older daughter Kristin mentioning what she calls "her angels" who appear to her as sparkling lights. She has seen "orbs" with her physical eyes all of her life, although she hadn't specifically used the word "orb" to describe them. As her mother, I believed her when she told me she was seeing something, yet I had a strong skeptical side that caused me to wonder if what she was seeing was real. Since I couldn't see them, a part of me didn't know if what she was describing really existed. Now I had seen one with my own eyes and I knew it was real.

Ashlee

Kristin reminded me of an experience her best friend Ashlee Yates had with a ball of light while they were in college. When I spoke with Ashlee, she said:

> When we were roommates in college, I awoke one night unexpectedly. I am a deep sleeper and never wake during the night. I was occupying the bottom bunk and as I opened my eyes, across the room to my right there appeared a ball of light. It was about the size of a tennis ball and pale golden yellow in color. I blinked a few times to clear my eyes, thinking it would disappear. I wasn't terrified by its appearance, just uneasy. (See Photo 67)

> I called out to Kristin to tell her what was happening. She sleepily answered that it was my guardian angel. I closed my eyes and tried to make it go away but it felt as if it wanted to be seen. When I opened my eyes, it was suddenly right in front of me. It hovered a foot from my face. I could see squiggly lines radiating out from it like a sunburst.

> Then I reached out to touch it and was surprised that my hand went right through it. It then faded away as if it were getting smaller and smaller. That was the first and only time I have seen it.

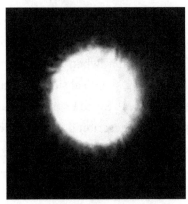

Photo 67 © Naomi Fugiwara. A pale
golden yellow orb with radiating squiggly
lines similar to Ashlee's orb.

Ashlee's story started me thinking. I wondered if I had any more photos with orbs. As I began sifting through years of old photos, I found some pictures with orbs pre-dating Chris's death, including a picture of my son and me surrounded by these light beings.

They were intriguing, but it wasn't until the spring of 2009 that I began seriously photographing orbs. One evening the sudden urge to grab my camera overwhelmed me. I turned my flash from "auto" to "on" because I'd heard this made it easier to capture the orbs in photos. I started to take pictures and discovered my living room was filled with orbs.

Excitedly, I called Kristin and told her about the orb photos I had just captured.

"Did you get any colored orbs?" she asked.

"They come in colors?" I dropped the phone and ran outside into the dark. My first shot captured two orbs. One was deep blue and the other was a dark golden color.

I was hooked!

The beautiful colors and numbers of orbs that began to appear in my photos were startling. I had seen photos of orbs in the few books published on the topic and on websites. The majority was taken outside in the dark. As I began to photograph them outside, I

36

wondered if they could just as easily come inside. I learned that indeed they could. In fact, from the comfort of my living room sofa, I was getting great pictures of hundreds of orbs.

As a grieving parent, I was filled with joy and excitement each time I photographed them. I delighted in their presence yet I didn't understand why their presence had such an impact on me emotionally, and *why* I was so thrilled and comforted by their appearance. They gave me hope that I wasn't alone and there was truly something more to life than what I could see. All the while, I continued to wonder if they weren't somehow connected to my son. Were other people experiencing this same phenomenon? More importantly, were there stories and experiences that linked orbs to the human soul?

Tracey

Tracey Buchanan is a forty-two year old Waldorf Method teacher and Senior Care provider living in the mountains of Colorado. She shared an experience she had as a child about her memories and experiences on the other side before she incarnated. She first describes herself as a bluish orb then she suddenly finds herself in a little girl's body, knowing she had made an agreement to do so. Tracey says:

> My earliest memory is of floating through the clouds to the Earth with many other rainbow colored orbs (myself included; I was a clear/bluish orb), healing fallen human soldiers on the ground or taking their souls away into the clouds.

> There was beautiful choir music all about us. I can remember this music, and it makes me cry with a longing I don't understand. The tones are irreproducible as far as I can fathom. At any rate, we were going about this work when suddenly I found myself in the body of a little girl, many miles away. I couldn't fly anymore and it confused me. Then I remembered that this was an agreement that the girl and I

had entered into and that it was "my turn" to do this, whatever "this" was.

My companions floated away into an orb-filled cloud, and I was very, very sad. I tried to follow, but I found my agreement would not let me. As a little girl, I was gently rocked to sleep in my bed every night by an unseen force I knew to be my angel. My angel would share symbols with me before I could read, the most important being the symbol of the human heartbeat, the Tau. I still have a heavy connection with it today.

When I was nine, I was allowed to hear the celestial music again and it created great awe and longing and fear in me. I asked it to stop, and said I was not ready to hear it, and it went away. Since then I have gravitated toward healing others.

Tracey's story was the first step in validating my intuition about orbs and their connection to the human soul. Had others who had also suffered a loss of a loved one experienced similar contact with a light being? I thought back to what Mandi Paterson (Christopher's best friend) and her mother experienced the weekend of my son's death.

Both Mandi and her mother, Barbara, were awakened in the middle of the night by a bright light, but a thorough investigation of the house had produced no clues about the source of the light. Later, they both felt it had something to do with Chris. Was it a common occurrence to have a ball of light appear after the loss of a loved one?

Bob

Bob Fairchild contacted me through my website and shared a story about his orb encounter just after the death of his beloved wife. Bob writes:

My wife and soul mate of thirty-five years passed away from colon cancer on November 5, 2012 in Kemptville, Ontario

Canada. We had conversations before her cancer diagnosis about leaving signs for the other—whoever went first. It was important for each of us to know if there was something beyond death.

After my wife passed, I made a deal with my two children: a daughter aged twenty-six and pregnant, and a son aged twenty-four, that we would all sleep together in my king sized bed for a few nights, and that if anyone was awake and couldn't sleep, we would talk.

It was for more my benefit than my children as I was having some problems with nighttime panic attacks, which ensued a few weeks before my wife's passing. I was only too glad to have someone to talk to. That night my son and I awoke and started talking.

About thirty minutes into the conversation, we experienced an earth tremor. My senses were on high alert because of this as I continued to talk with my son. We did not want to wake my daughter as she had been through a rough day and needed her sleep. About twenty minutes after the earth tremor, I happened to notice something out of the corner of my eye.

I have lived in this house and slept in this same bedroom for twenty-seven years. It is out in the country and surrounded by a mature forest of maples and hemlock trees and far from any source of light. What I saw was a single brilliant disk of light about four inches in diameter over my wife's closet door. Our walls are dark green with white pine wainscoting. The intensity of light was consistent from the center of the disk to the edge and did not luminesce beyond the edge of the disk. The color was white with a little bit of yellow.

Following the appearance of this disk, a second one appeared which slightly overlapped the first, followed by a third and then a fourth disk: each of which overlapped the previous. The total appearance was very much like the symbol used by Audi cars with the four overlapping circles.

After the fourth circle appeared, all four circles disappeared together. The whole scene lasted about three seconds. I asked my son if he saw this but unfortunately, he had closed his eyes and was starting to doze during the interruption in our conversation.

I saw the same event later in the morning just before the sun came up, but the intensity of the light was diminished and the circles disappeared individually and not at the same time after the appearance of the fourth disk. I compared the brilliance of this light to a high intensity LED flashlight that I held close to the wall trying but unable to get that level of brilliance. There was no beam of light that emitted into our bedroom and what I saw was not from any outside source.

All I know is that I no longer have any doubt that there is something beyond death and that death is not an endpoint in our lives but a passage to something else. I am still trying to understand the meaning of this. I have no photographs but I know what I saw and it has changed the way I view life.

Touched by Bob's story and the synchronicity of the lights appearing just after his wife had passed, I was also delighted to know that I hadn't just imagined the orb in my bedroom. Could the lights we saw be related to both Bob's wife and my son? Were there other stories about a ball of light appearing during grief?

Alan

In March of 2015, I was contacted by Alan Bird who lives in Surrey, England. He shared a story similar to Bob Fairchild's story after his wife crossed over from cancer. Alan says:

My wife died on the March 10, 2014 after a short, but immensely brave battle with late stage cervical cancer. We had been married for forty-seven years and fourteen days. Three or four weeks before her demise she said to me, "I'll never leave you Alan" and I often draw on that when my spirit is low.

A couple of months after her spirit was set free, I witnessed the following events. It was around 10:30 pm and I was about to get into bed. I was standing at the foot of the bed and as I turned to get into "my" side of the bed I noticed "something white" on the floor about halfway along and at the side of the bed (the bedroom lights were off and the only light in the room was natural light from outside). My immediate thought was this is a piece of fur from my ginger and white cat but, as I took a step forward, the "something white" suddenly transformed into a spinning circle of light (about the size of a tennis ball), it was three or four inches above the carpeted floor and had other circles of light within it. The whole "event" lasted for about five seconds and I was rooted to the spot while this was taking place.

I feel privileged to have witnessed this phenomenon and know what I would like it to be, but I haven't got a clue. Also, I have done a little reading concerning "orbs" but they have always been described as solid balls of light whereas "my orb" was "see through" and resembled an "armillary sphere."

The Reyes

Jim and Anne Reyes had a sighting in their home that they couldn't explain. Anne writes:

My mother-in-law had died about ten days prior to this sighting. My husband Jim was sitting at the dining room table, I was standing. I turned around, looked up, and saw a perfectly white light about the size of a large dinner plate. I walked over to look and saw this opaque orb and it suddenly changed before our eyes. It looked like clouds were moving quickly through it from left to right. Then suddenly it just got small and then disappeared! We believe this had something to do with our mother's spirit.

Sandy

Christmas 2015 brought an unusual gift to Sandy Arsenault Panek and her husband, one she believes came from her son PJ who crossed over in 2011 from a boating accident.

> On December 26, 2015, my husband and I were playing bingo with our grandson. It was a rainy cold evening when I heard my front door rattle like someone was trying to enter our home, but no one came in so we ignored it. Then it happened again. I said to my husband, "It sounds like someone is at the door. Did you hear that?"
>
> He had heard what I had heard. I checked the front door and no one was there. But when I returned to the bingo game we were playing, I felt there was a presence around us. After my grandson left for the evening to go home with his dad, I decided to sit out on my front porch. That's when I noticed a "phosphorescent" ball of light the size of a large egg perched on the tip of a tree branch, just sitting there glowing a luminescent green.
>
> I looked to see if it could be a star or a planet shining down, but it wasn't in the sky. The ball of light was resting on the tree branch, just glowing. I tapped on my bay window to get my husband's attention to signal for him to have a look. He quickly came out and was witnessing the same phenomenon with me. He went to get his binoculars to have a closer look. It was a glowing ball sitting in the tree. No evidence of any glow bugs in that ball of light.
>
> I looked up phosphorus light emitting from plants, but it only had scientific explanations about a plant glowing. The whole tree wasn't glowing. Phosphorus lights only glow in warmer temperatures. It was not warm out last night.

Could this have been a visit from my deceased son? First the door rattling, then the feeling of a presence then the glowing ball of light? I would like to believe we had a visit from him. This morning I went outside and took my binoculars out. There is no evidence of a firefly nest. There was nothing there today to explain what we saw.

Anne

Reverend Anne Puryear co-founded the Spiritual Science Research Center in Washington, D.C. After moving to Phoenix in 1977, she served for four years as Director of the Department of Spiritual Healing at the A.R.E. Medical Clinic, the Medical Research Division of the Edgar Cayce Foundation. Trained in Gestalt and other therapies, she often counsels with suicidal children and adults, and survivors of suicide. Both she and her husband, Herb Puryear, are the founders of the International Conference on After-Death Communication, and The Logos Center in Scottsdale, Arizona.

Anne is the author of *Stephen Lives: His Life, Suicide and Afterlife*.[22] *Stephen Lives* is "a journey of faith and hope, revealing universal truths of life, death and the afterlife that comfort and inspire all who journey with them."[23] I cried as I read this heart-wrenching story. I felt as if I knew this family intimately, especially Stephen. Anne's pain, heartache, grief and frustration had been my own. In Anne, I realized that I had found a kindred spirit.

As I read on, Anne revealed her connection to spirit and began to communicate with Stephen after his death. She mentions that one evening as she sat meditating, a large sphere of brilliant white light entered the room. She writes:

Within moments, across the room, there appeared a sphere of white light in front of the wall, about eight or ten feet away. It was a glowing, brilliant light. I started to sit up; but I couldn't move. Though I was propped on the arm of the couch, with my head tilted to the left side, I could see the form as if I were sitting up straight.

Try as I might, I could move no part of my body. A peaceful feeling came over me. This being of light did not communicate with words or even thoughts, but I felt totally at peace and at one with it. It stayed almost fifteen minutes and then disappeared. I could move my body again and I sat up. I questioned in my mind what had happened. I could not deny the incredible peace I felt. I knew that God was answering my prayers.

Only a few minutes later, the being of light appeared again. As before, I could not move, but this time I was sitting up. It stayed about ten minutes before disappearing. More of His healing and peace and love and light filled my whole body. When He left, I knew that Jesus had been with me.

Later, I called Anne and asked her several questions about the sphere of light. I asked her if she had ever considered that what she had seen thirty years ago might have been an orb. She said it had never crossed her mind but that's exactly what it was. She mentioned that it was eighteen to twenty-four inches in diameter, and so bright you almost couldn't look at it. It appeared to her twice.

These stories validated what my intuition had already told me; the balls of light or orbs were in some way connected to Spirit and our loved ones. Now I needed to prove this supposition through investigation and research.

If I could prove what my intuition was telling me, then I wouldn't be separated from my son: I would know that he still lives on. Next to having Chris back in the flesh, this would be the greatest comfort I could experience.

Each night, I started with the same routine of taking orb photos. From that time on, orbs became a daily part of my life. They were on my mind from the moment I woke up until I fell asleep. I talked about them constantly and spent hours on the Internet in search of photos, stories and information about this phenomenon.

Almost on a daily basis, I experienced a connection to Spirit, whether it was through orbs or after-death communication (ADCs). Yet in spite of these amazing experiences, the skeptical part of me continued to question if what I was experiencing was real or merely a symptom of my grief.

Was I creating this myth myself about this spiritual connection, simply to compensate for my loss—was this a type of desperation related to deep, unresolved grieving, or was I having authentic experiences? Was my intuition correct and somehow these orbs were related to the human soul or consciousness? If they were real, were they giving me another clue about the survival of consciousness?

CHAPTER FOUR

"Find a place inside where there is joy
and the joy will burn out the pain."

~ Joseph Campbell

Embrace the Gift

The more I tuned into my inner guidance and connected to God, Source and I AM Presence, the greater my desire to listen and look for Spirit. It was as if my son's death had turned on my spiritual awareness. The messages were everywhere; I just needed to pay attention. This tenuous thread was a lifeline that often rescued me from the sadness and grief.

As I began to keep a journal of these experiences, they reminded me that I was not separate from Spirit or my son, but a part of both. These precious moments carried me through those times when I thought I could no longer carry myself. They came in different ways and at different times. I realized I was not to judge the process, but to embrace each experience as a precious gift from God.

Whenever I stood steadfast in my intuitive *knowing* that we live on after-death, it seemed I was rewarded by contact with my son and Spirit. I experienced hundreds of after-death communications. I felt Chris's touch and presence, had visions and vivid dreams, experienced electrical phenomena, unusual animal encounters and synchronistic events; and heard a voice that saved me from serious injury. The validation from those precious moments gave me relief from the physical and emotional pain of grief.

With each spiritual experience, another tiny piece of me healed. With great anticipation, I looked forward to these connections with my son.

Valentine's Day

As the five-year anniversary of my son's death approached, I realized that friends, family and I had had so many after-death communication experiences with my son Christopher that I decided to write a book about them. I wanted the people who were closest to me to read the wonderful stories as a reminder of the miracle of Spirit in our lives.

There was no hurry or deadline. My intention wasn't to heal myself per se, but to share my story with others, hoping it might ease their pain if they had experienced similar losses.

In January 2011, I spent two weeks working on the manuscript, feeling excited and motivated. Then suddenly I fell into a deep depression. I had never felt like this before. Through my writing, I was reliving Chris's accident. I missed my son and writing about him made our physical separation all too real. As I continued to write down the moving experiences of contact with Spirit, I fell deeper into a place I had yet to venture. It was the hole of despair, which was always to my left, just inches from a misstep.

At a certain point, I stopped writing and moped around in my pajamas, not leaving the house for days at a time. I didn't tell my family how I felt, although my youngest daughter Olivia noticed. The pain was overwhelming and debilitating. I just didn't want to be here anymore. It hurt too much.

The sadness was so deep and profound. I missed seeing my son in person. I'd had five years to watch the aftermath of his devastating accident unfold in front of me. If I could get my daughter Olivia to stop by the grocery store or a fast food restaurant on her way home from school, she would at least have something to eat for dinner.

Honestly, I wasn't up to preparing a meal for her, although without fail, every day of her life I have made her school lunch and continued to do so during this time. I always felt it was important to say goodbye to her as she left for school each day. It was a dark time for me and I stopped taking orb photos. This confirmation of their presence had always filled me with joy. In fact, Olivia would often tease me, saying that I loved the orbs more than I loved her.

That's not true, of course, but they are infinitely entertaining to watch as they zoom around the room illuminated by the infrared light on my camera. I usually laugh and tease them, and in return, they've given me some beautiful pictures. This time, however, even the orbs weren't able to lift my spirits.

As I sat moping on the couch watching TV, the lamp over the bar started to flicker. I knew Spirit was trying to get my attention, but I ignored the sign. It just didn't matter. My son was gone and he was never coming back. The flickering continued off and on for a while until finally I said aloud, "Okay already, I'll take the darn pictures!" Half-heartedly, I took several photos and tossed the camera back on the coffee table.

Usually I reviewed my pictures. This time I didn't bother. Several days later, when I finally recovered from my waning interest in the orbs, I scrolled back through the photos and noticed a beautiful pink orb by my angel in the living room, just a few feet away from the flickering lamp over the bar. It was date stamped February 14, Valentine's Day. (Photo 68)

The orb near the angel was significant to me because I always see her as the Angel of Love and Protection for my house. She brings peace and tranquility to my surroundings. When I think of her, I think of my son in Heaven. It was difficult having these experiences and sharing them with friends and family when no one else, except for my girls, sccmcd excited about them.

My only guidance and support were the few published books on orbs. Klaus Heinemann, Ph.D., co-author of *Orbs: Their Mission & Message of Hope* states, "It is our position, then, that orbs appear in meaningful places in photographs, and not haphazardly; it is because they are there by design."[24]

Photo 68 (left). Valentine's Day Orb 2011. Photo 69 (right). Blue orb appears with same angel June 16, 2011. © Virginia Hummel.

The pink orb had appeared for a reason. My intuition told me that Chris was connected to it. I knew he felt my sorrow and wanted to send me some love. It was his way of saying, "Mom, get up off the couch, stop moping, and find the joy that you feel when you take orb photos."

He was right. It was just what I needed to lift my spirits. I felt closer to my son and connected to God when I felt joy. Joseph Campbell said, "Find a place inside where there's joy and the joy will burn out the pain."[25] I never realized the wisdom of those well-chosen words until I discovered that my joy regarding the orb phenomenon helped me transmute the pain of my grief.

The appearance of the pink orb was not a coincidence; instead, I believe it was connected with my son. This was a significant experience for me in my grief journey and I wondered if anyone else was experiencing this kind of connection with orbs.

Nancy – Visiting Orbs

Nancy Myers is the author of *Entering the Light Fantastic*. She has also embraced the orb phenomenon after the death of her son, Robbie, and discovered the healing power of their presence. She has taken some wonderful photos of orbs in meaningful places. It was through my website and the orb phenomenon that we met.

While visiting Nancy in the fall of 2012, she suddenly stated she could feel the presence of both of our boys. Grabbing her camera, she directed her husband Rob and me toward the back of the room. I laughed and told the boys to jump into the shot, fully expecting them to do so.

Photo 70 (left) © Nancy Myers. Virginia Hummel and Rob Myers after requesting our sons to appear. Photo 71 (right) © Nancy Myers. An orb appears after requesting an orb photo for a Christmas card.

In Photo 70 appear two large orbs, one above Rob and me, along with several smaller ones. Is it a coincidence to find two "dust" spots positioned just above our heads in a meaningful place in the photo?

According to Klaus Heinemann, Ph.D., co-author of *The Orb Project*, "Airborne particles should always be in statistically random locations; the orbs would then have to be expected to show up in photos in statistically random locations—almost *never* in "meaningful" locations."[26]

During the Holiday season of 2012, Nancy Myers grabbed her camera and stepped outside to her front yard. She had just asked Spirit for an orb photo for her Christmas card when she snapped this shot. (Photo 71)

It still makes me smile to see it. Is it Santa or better yet her son, Robbie, with a sense of humor? We may never know the real answer, but regardless of the identity of this soul, this photo stimulates our imagination and offers us the opportunity to make that leap of faith to reach out and connect with Spirit.

Were Nancy and I the only two who were experiencing orbs in meaningful places, or were they also appearing to others who had lost family or friends?

Debra

Debra Tuohy was a Facebook friend who always posted the most inspirational quotes and pictures while grieving her daughter, Shayna. I looked forward to opening my Facebook page each morning and reading her uplifting posts. She passed away less than a year after her daughter crossed. Her sister captured an orb near a memorial spot in their garden just after Shayna's funeral. (Photo 72) Along with the bright orb, notice the heart shape on the tree that happened to appear just after Shayna's death.

Patricia

My good friend Patricia Alexander, award-winning co-author of *The Book of Comforts: Simple, Powerful Ways to Comfort Your Spirit, Body and Soul*, lost her beloved husband and soul mate, Michael Burgos, in August of 2011.[27] The following month I introduced her to the world of orbs, when I met her for the first time at a writers' Conference.

Since then, she has faithfully photographed an orb in her bedroom as she calls out to Michael to say goodnight. Patricia says that during this time of grief and adjustment, her connection with Michael through the presence of an orb has given her a sense of solace unlike any other. On a trip to present her first keynote address after Michael's death, Patricia took a few pictures in her hotel room. She took seven pictures and was surprised that none of them contained orbs. She had fully expected Michael to be there with her on the eve of her first speech since his passing. Undaunted, she called out to Michael and said, "I'm not going to stop taking orb pictures until you go over there right now and sit on my suitcase."

Photo 72 (left) © Debra Tuohy. An orb appears at a memorial site.
Photo 73 (right) © Patricia Alexander. An orb appears when a deceased husband is requested to sit on a suitcase.

Photo 73 is what she captured after calling out to her husband. Michael had a sense of humor in life and apparently also in death. In the three years since her husband's transition, Patricia has been deeply focused on orbs. Above all, she remains open to the miracles possible through a connection with Spirit.

Carol – More Validation

Carol Danforth, R.N., shares a story in which she specifically asked a particular individual to appear as an orb. Carol says:

On a very slow Sunday afternoon on the neonatal intensive care unit floor of the hospital, I let my thoughts drift to Dr. Mike, a much-loved pediatrician who worked with the children and nurses on my floor. He had taken his own life a year earlier while suffering from end stage cancer. He loved children. I wondered if he was still present on the ward and would appear for me as an orb.

I pulled out my camera and stood in the hallway facing a small waiting area. "Dr. Mike," I said, "If you're here, I want you to sit in the middle chair." I was delighted to see an orb hovering above the middle chair. (Photo 74) I hurried to the other nurses and showed them the photo. All of them except one were amazed.

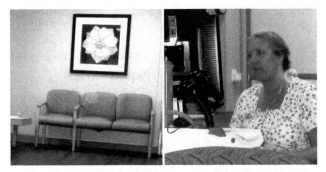

Photo 74 (left). An orb appears in the center seat after requesting deceased Dr. Mike to sit there. Photo 75 (right). An orb appears after requesting Dr. Mike to sit on her left shoulder. © Carol Danforth.

"I don't believe it," said the skeptical nurse.

"It's true. I asked Dr. Mike to sit in the middle chair. It's him." I pointed to the orb again.

The skeptical nurse sat at her desk. "I don't believe it. Dr. Mike, if you're here, you sit your butt on my left shoulder right now." Carol snapped the picture. (Photo 75) What are the odds that a single dust spot would happen to appear on the nurse's shoulder, positioned in a meaningful place in the photo?

Aunt Susan "Mimi"

My Aunt Susan passed away from cancer on March 15, 2015. Susan was a terrific hostess, wife and mother of five children and nine grandchildren. A week later, her family gathered with ours at an intimate memorial dinner we gave for them to honor their mother.

Her family knew that I took orb pictures but I don't think they ever really paid much attention to my work. Through my orb photography, I realized that I could give them an opportunity to experience firsthand this miraculous phenomenon and a connection to their mother in the afterlife.

The following photos surprised even me at how easily our family on the other side wants to communicate with us. Coincidently, my Aunt Carol also had cancer and crossed over the day of the party.

My cousin, Virginia Dirschl, shared a favorite poem of her mother's during the memorial dinner when I captured orb Photo 76. After seeing the photo, many of her family agreed that the orb had to have been Susan. Then as my cousin Kirk stood to remember his mother, I captured Photo 77.

Photo 76 (left). An orb appear after a favorite poem is read. Photo 77 (right). Two bright orbs during a memorial dinner. Photos © Virginia Hummel.

For me and the others at the party who saw the photo, it was obvious to all of us that both Aunt Susan and Aunt Carol were there with us in spirit. I noticed that these photos gave them something to focus on other than their loss. They created curiosity and excitement along with the possibility that there really was something beyond death. Somehow, part of us lived on.

When I found Lillie, my Aunt Susan's wonderful caregiver, who was by Susan's side for over a year and the moment she crossed, and my sister-in-law sitting together just after our dinner I said, "Let me see if I can take a picture of you both with Aunt Susan." I called out to Susan to join them. I captured Photo 78. Later in the evening my Aunt Susan's daughter-in-law, Caroline, asked me if I would be able to take a photo of her with "Mimi" as an orb.

Photo 78 (left). An orb appears after requesting my aunt to join in the photo. Photo 79 (right). Caroline Pereira asked for "Mimi" to appear as an orb at her left shoulder. © Virginia Hummel

When I showed her the picture I captured she got excited and said that she hadn't said anything but that she had secretly asked for "Mimi" to appear as an orb at her shoulder. (Photo 79) The part of me that is still skeptical these kinds of photos are possible must concede that the coincidence, position and timing of these orb photos, especially in light of the fact these shots were requested of our loved ones and spirit, are compelling.

Most importantly, I witnessed how my Aunt Susan's family felt when I showed them the photos at the party. They were excited and joyful at a time when loss can weigh so heavy on our hearts. Even my staunchly skeptical Uncle Bill began to lean a little closer to embracing the orb phenomenon as a connection to our loved ones. These photos and stories validated the experiences I was having with orbs. The idea that the orbs were connected to our loved ones was beginning to make sense and I wasn't the only one who thought so.

As I continued to photograph orbs, I noticed that my excitement and joy would immediately encourage more of them to appear. I also discovered that whenever I summoned orbs to appear, either by thinking about them or by verbally asking them to show up, they did. It was almost as if I had radar or some type of antenna that sent out a signal and they responded. The orbs were exhibiting a consciousness.

Stunned by this discovery, I knew I needed definitive answers when I began to talk to them and they reacted. How was this possible? Did I possess some magical ability to interact with Spirit, or had I tapped into a God-given ability innate in each of us?

CHAPTER FIVE

"The light of the body is in the eye therefore thy eye be single, thy
whole body shall be full of light."

~ Matthew 6:22

DMT: The Spirit Molecule (N, N-Dimethyltryptamine)

You may have heard stories about people who have had a miraculous
experience with Spirit, visions of the Virgin Mary, an angel that arrives
in time to save a life, the deep, rich and hyper-real experiences of a
near-death occurrence, or visions, voices and signs of deceased loved
ones.

Why does this happen to some people and not to others? Are they
special, or is something else at work that creates the opportunity for
these experiences?

As I started to seek answers to these questions, one particular
explanation jumped off the page. Perhaps the communication or
response is facilitated by DMT, a chemical produced by the pineal
gland, a small pinecone shaped gland located in the center of the brain
between the left and right hemispheres.[28] This location coincidentally
aligns with the Hindu concept of the third eye, a spot above and
between the eyebrows.[29]

The third eye is a mystical concept that relates to higher
consciousness, insight and enlightenment. It is also associated with

precognition, clairvoyance and out of body experiences (OBE). The third eye is sometimes referred to as the mind's eye.[30]

The pineal gland is also in alignment with the crown chakra at the top of the head.[31] The term "chakra," which is derived from the traditional Hindu system of medicine, refers to a spinning vortex of colored energy located in one of the seven spiritual centers of the human body.[32] René Descartes, a French philosopher, identified the pineal gland as the "seat of the soul."[33] Plato referred to this gland as the eye of wisdom.[34]

Photo 80 © Marlon Brammer. An orb appears at the third eye of a Buddhist monk.

DMT is found throughout nature and occurs in trace amounts in humans and mammals. For centuries, indigenous cultures, including Amazon natives, South American Shamans and American Indians have consumed ayahuasca and peyote (a plant based DMT) to achieve altered states, healing, and to connect with the Divine.[35]

During the early nineties, Dr. Rick Strassman conducted clinical research at the University of New Mexico by injecting volunteers with DMT or N, N-Dimethyltryptamine. He has written a book on the subject titled, *DMT: The Spirit Molecule,* which, according to the publisher, "makes the bold case that DMT, naturally released by the pineal gland, facilitates the soul's movement in and out of the body and is an integral part of the birth and death experiences, as well as the highest states of meditation."[36]

Although Dr. Strassman injected his volunteers with DMT, which created spiritual experiences, millions of other people have had similar experiences naturally. Meditation is known to produce effects similar to DMT, i.e. the ability to access different types of spiritual experiences. It is believed that the utterance of sacred words, chanting, breathing and sound or visualization techniques used in mediation can alter brain wave function, raising the vibration of the pineal gland and stimulating the release of DMT.[37]

Listening to audio or audio-visual recordings has also been known to passively produce transpersonal experiences that deal with states or areas of consciousness beyond the limits of personal identity.[38]

If DMT is the foundation for spiritually transformative experiences (STEs), could it also have been a catalyst for my ability to experience an almost daily connection with Spirit, and on occasion physically see orbs after my son crossed? Strassman's research shows that stress affects the release of DMT. Because the pineal gland is separate from the brain and protected by the blood-brain barrier, the pineal is not affected by adrenaline released by the adrenal glands: the fight or flight mechanism. Instead, the pineal gland is affected by the surge of adrenaline and non-adrenaline released by the pineal nerve endings.[39]

Could the extraordinary stress of my grief have altered my ability to secrete more DMT at specific times? During my early stages of grief, I felt as if I were physically vibrating. The more I thought about Spirit and contact with my son, the more joyful and euphoric I felt. The more joy I felt, the stronger the vibration in my body. Regarding the volunteers in his DMT research project, Strassman reports that "nearly everyone remarked on the 'vibrations' brought on by DMT, the sense of powerful energy pulsing through them at a very rapid and high frequency."[40]

At times, I am able to recreate this state and recognize the same incredible feeling of vibration. This is when I also experience increased ability to manifest the things upon which I focus. I describe this feeling as "swimming in champagne" or "getting ready to be shot out into the Universe." This experience can be also compared to the visceral feeling one receives from the vibration of a jet plane during takeoff, as the throttle pushes toward maximum thrust.

Kuan Yin

During the first few weeks following the death of my son, I experienced almost daily contact with Spirit. It was also a time when I felt as if I were constantly swimming in champagne. An incident that was particularly interesting occurred one evening less than two weeks after his accident. That morning I had an unusual experience with flickering lights in my house and knew without a doubt that it was Christopher. I could feel how these events energized and affected the vibration in my body, which seemed to increase my spiritual experiences and ease my grief. The following is an excerpt from my book, *Miracle Messenger.*[41]

> That evening, my eleven-year-old daughter Olivia came to me too frightened to sleep in her own room. The story of [contact with my son through] the flickering lights that morning had unsettled her, so I allowed her to crawl into bed next to me. In my nightstand drawer, I had placed the small book of spiritual prayers that I'd given to Chris years earlier. I found it in his own nightstand the weekend of his death when we cleaned out his room.
>
> I cradled the worn dog-eared pages against my heart for a moment as if somehow they would help me gain a small connection to him. Then I read aloud for twenty minutes, sometimes repeating the same verse over and over, more for my own well-being than for my daughter's, I suppose.
>
> Even though my first thought as a mother was to comfort and calm my little girl, I soon found myself melding with the words. They came alive on the page, their meaning tangible

as they rolled off my tongue until my daughter drifted off to sleep and my lids grew weary. I fell asleep remembering the excitement of the lights in the laundry room that morning and the anticipation of another contact with my son.

In the middle of the night, I awoke abruptly. Someone was in my room. Terrified, I lay on my right side with both hands tucked beneath my cheek and peered from the blankets that partially covered my head. I tried to move but was paralyzed. My heart pounded as adrenaline shot through my body.

Olivia lay next to me, still asleep. I couldn't even turn my head to see who might be standing next to her, much less try to save our lives. I lay motionless and listened intently for sounds of the intruder. My mind raced with what to do next.

Photo 81 © Virginia Hummel. An orb similar to the glittering white lights.

As I stared past my nightstand to the narrow wall at the entrance to my bathroom, I noticed a small gathering of glittering white lights. I blinked to focus on what I was seeing. Was I awake or dreaming? I pinched my palm. I was awake.

The glittering white lights danced on my wall in an area the size of a dinner plate. (Photo 81) They reminded me of strong sunlight on rippling water, although I didn't need to squint from their brightness to see them. I held my breath as they performed their shimmering dance and watched as they shifted from silver to gold. It was like watching the dazzling gold glitters from Fourth of July fireworks.

As I lay quietly watching the lights, I forgot about a possible intruder. Then the lights turned from gold to sparkling translucent red chips about the size of a deck of cards. The lights encompassed the entire wall.

Mesmerized by the sheer wonder of it, there was no reflection from these lights anywhere else in the bedroom. My mind raced for an explanation. The most rational one I could come up with was that a police car with its flashing red light was in my back yard. The red light must be filtering through my blackout drapes and reflecting on the wall in front of me.

The moment I realized that scenario was impossible, fear shot through me once again. I knew that what I was witnessing was not of this Earth. Never at any time did I feel afraid of the lights, but what I felt instead was fear of the unknown. As spiritual as I thought I was, nothing had prepared me for my reaction. It was too much for me to process.

In the next instant, the sparkling red lights vanished. I lay motionless for several minutes, attempting to recall every detail of the experience. I reached out for Olivia, breathing peacefully, and then lay awake for hours peeking out from beneath my covers. I was frightened, curious, and determined as I examined every scenario I could imagine, desperate for an explanation of what I had seen.

Ultimately, I could find none other than the reality that Spirit had visited me. It was one of the many profound events in my life. For the time being, I concluded that the lights were my son in Spirit. The next day I was so excited and couldn't wait to tell everyone about the lights. Some loved the story and were really excited. This small group of friends and family who had had such experiences themselves were open to such possibilities. Others, of course, thought I was nuts.

For the next six months, I firmly believed it had been my son's presence in my room that night. I clung to that belief until I came upon a book by Doreen Virtue, Ph.D., titled *Archangels and Ascended Masters.*[42] Casually, I flipped through the pages and stopped when I came to a section about the Eastern Goddess named Kuan Yin. I began to read. I had no idea who Kuan Yin was and had never heard of her before now:

She is one of the most beloved and popular Goddesses of compassion and protection, and her name means "She who hears prayers." You may see the color red when she's around, such as red sparkles of light or a red mist that appears out of nowhere.[43]

Could it have been Kuan Yin who visited me with her sparkling red lights after I had delivered my heartfelt prayers? It had been twelve days since Chris had crossed over.

As a mother, I was still in a state of disbelief and shock. Waves of sadness washed over me as I contemplated never seeing or touching his physical form again. I allowed those moments of grief to rise, crest and recede, sometimes rushing them along because the thought of another moment of contact with my son brought relief and joy.

My whole body tingled for months as I seemed to be half caught between worlds. It was that "walking on air" feeling that nothing can touch you and everything else before that time seemed dull and void of life. I was floating somewhere above our human earthly existence, but not quite in the other one.[44]

As I look back, it was quite possible that I was in an altered state created by my highly sensitized physical and emotional condition, similar to what Dr. Strassman's volunteers experienced when injected with DMT.

Was this altered state a direct result of DMT? As humans, are we able to control the release of DMT, either consciously or unconsciously, as a God-given mechanism guaranteed to facilitate a connection to levels of consciousness outside of our own?

CHAPTER SIX

"The orb acted as a kind of an interpreter between me and this
extraordinary presence surrounding me."

~ Eben Alexander, M.D.

Survival of Consciousness

The scientific community has long clung to the reductionist theory
that the brain creates consciousness, and if the brain dies,
consciousness dies along with it.[45] Science has also held that near-
death experiences, hallucinations, dreamlike states or so-called
spiritual experiences are brain dependent. In spite of these traditional
beliefs, however, a growing number of doctors and scientists are
acknowledging that consciousness survives death.

Eben

In 2008, Dr. Eben Alexander suffered a near-death experience (NDE)
caused by an extremely rare illness called *E. coli* bacterial meningitis.
As he lay deep in coma and on a ventilator, his neo-cortex, the part of
the brain that makes us human and creates thought, was rendered
useless.

As a highly-trained neurosurgeon who has operated on thousands
of patients, Dr. Alexander would have previously been one of the first
to explain that NDEs are "fantasies caused by the brain under extreme

stress." *E. coli* bacterial meningitis is typically fatal. In Alexander's case, his illness was so severe his doctors believed that if he lived he would most likely spend the rest of his life in a "persistent vegetative state."[46] That he survived his illness and returned with his memory intact is hailed as a medical miracle.

Eben Alexander's number one *New York Times* bestselling book, *Proof of Heaven: A Neurosurgeon's Journey into the Afterlife*, details his journey into "the deepest realms of super-physical existence." He is escorted through his near-death experience by a beautiful angelic being: a girl with golden brown hair and sparkling blue eyes. She accompanies Alexander as they ride on the tip of a butterfly wing through a world that was "vibrant, ecstatic and stunning."[47]

At another point during his NDE, Dr. Alexander finds himself in a black womb-like void. It was filled with a brilliant light that emanated from an orb. The void was the presence of God whom Dr. Alexander refers to as "Om." He says, "The orb acted as a kind of an interpreter between me and this extraordinary presence surrounding me…the orb, who remained in some way connected to the Girl on the Butterfly Wing, who in fact was she, was guiding me through this process."[48]

Dr. Alexander says that after documenting his experience, he then sat down to research NDEs. He was dismayed to discover that most people encounter a family member or loved one during their near-death experience. As a neuroscientist, he questioned the validity of his experience because the only person he had encountered was a stranger. Shouldn't his father, who had recently passed, been present?

Alexander had been adopted as an infant. Four months after he had awakened from his coma, he received a photograph from his birth family. It was of his youngest sibling who had died ten-and-a-half years before Alexander's NDE. Her name was Betsy and someone whom Dr. Alexander had never met.

According to Alexander, the following day as he stared at her photo, the world of the Here and Now and the world of the Afterlife collided. "There was no mistaking her, no mistaking the loving smile, the confidant and infinitely comforting look, the sparkling blue eyes…" It was Betsy. She was the angelic being, the Girl on the Butterfly Wing. Betsy had accompanied him throughout his NDE and was the "orb" that acted as an interpreter in the void between Alexander and the presence of God.[49]

The neurosurgeon's NDE account confirmed what my five years of experience and research with orbs had shown me: not only does life continue after our physical death, but the consciousness of our loved ones can manifest as the appearance of a brilliant ball of light. I wept for ten minutes after reading this account.

My mind raced. If Betsy could manifest her consciousness as a brilliant ball of light, an orb—isn't it possible that Christopher may have appeared in the physical realm to visit me that night in 2007 in a similar form? If so, couldn't some of the orbs that are appearing in millions of photographs around the world be the manifestation of consciousness of other departed loved ones?

It was the connection and breakthrough I needed and validated my intuition that our soul or consciousness energy could manifest as a ball of light. I was excited about this revelation until I read further about DMT and learned that science and skeptics concluded that a DMT "dump" creates a near-death experience or brain-based hallucination. My heart sank. Suddenly, that little seed of doubt began to grow. How could I be sure that Alexander's NDE with Betsy was real and not a brain-based hallucination?

As I pondered this dilemma, it occurred to me that the problem with the reductionists' theory was the appearance of his birth sister, Betsy. Regardless of whether Dr. Alexander's consciousness remained intact and functioning inside or outside of his body, we do know that Betsy's consciousness had to have survived ten and a half years from her death in order to connect with her brother, who had never met her.

According to Dr. Alexander, his badly damaged neocortex precluded the regions of his brain associated with a DMT "dump" from generating the aural and visual experiences needed to support the theory of a brain dependent hallucination.

Near-death experiences occur when the body is under extreme stress of impending death. Dr. Strassman states: "Massive surges of stress hormones also mark the near-death experience...It may also be a time when the protective mechanisms of the pineal are flooded and otherwise inactive pathways to DMT production turned on."[50]

Was it possible that both Dr. Alexander and the skeptics were only partially correct in their assertions about DMT's role in his NDE. Science states that consciousness is brain-based and thus transpersonal experiences attributed to DMT must also be brain-based. Yet there is overwhelming evidence that consciousness exists outside the body and a growing number of doctors and scientists who support this conclusion, including Alexander. With this understanding, it is our responsibility to investigate other kinds of "fact-based science" that may also be incorrect including the role that DMT plays in our body.

Rick Strassman also says of his volunteers "there seemed to be a clearly identifiable sense of movement of consciousness away from the body, such as 'falling,' 'lifting up,' 'flying,' a feeling of weightlessness, or rapid movement."[51]

With that in mind, I wondered if DMT was present in Alexander and instead, acted as a booster to facilitate his experience that occurred outside his brain? According to Alexander he was in extreme pain prior to his coma. What if, in the early hours of Alexander's illness, stress caused by the extreme pain from the effects of the meningitis forced a DMT "dump?" This "dump" then acted as a catalyst for the soul and facilitated its departure from the human body much like a rocket booster launches a space shuttle into orbit.

It seems reasonable to conclude that the level of stress and pain I experienced after Chris crossed over was different from the extreme stress and pain endured by Alexander prior to his coma. Yet during my grief, I also experienced a connection with consciousness apart from my own. I knew my experiences were real. Were Dr. Alexander's also real?

Is it possible that DMT facilitated Dr. Alexander's near-death experience; an event that occurred outside his brain? Could DMT be God's way of insuring that the soul is reconnected with the Divine at the moment of impending physical death or other traumatic life events?

Harry

Were there other documented near-death experiences, similar to Dr. Alexander's, which also revealed unknown information that could be corroborated after the NDE?

Author Harry Hone suffered an NDE from cardiac arrest. He has documented his experience in his book, *The Light at the End of the Tunnel*.[52] Harry left his body in Newport Hospital and briefly watched the doctors working to revive him. He then traveled at high speed and was drawn into a dark tunnel where he could see at the end "the indescribable, effulgently pure white world of 'light.'"[53] He also realized that Harry Hone consists of a "tiny speck or spark of light" and the light had left its body or house."[54]

Something else also happened to Harry during his near-death experience. He received knowledge about his long-lost sister's whereabouts by a voice on the other side, which told him of her exact location. Separated as children during WWII, Harry and his sister hadn't seen each other for thirty-four years. They reunited after Harry's NDE. She was living in a country that was halfway around the world from his current home.[55]

George

P.M.H. Atwater is a noted authority on near-death experience and its after-effects. She is the author of fourteen books, including *Beyond the Light: What Isn't Being Said About Near-death Experience: from Visions of Heaven to Glimpses of Hell,* which describes the remarkable

NDE of George Rodonaia, Ph.D.[56] Rodonaia was an outspoken Soviet dissident and atheist who was murdered by the KGB. After being run over by a car three times and pronounced dead, his body lay inside a cooler in a morgue for three days, during which time he experienced a detailed near-death experience.

At one point during his NDE, he visited a newborn that cried continually. He communicated telepathically with the infant and learned of a broken hip that occurred during its birth. When doctors started to perform Rodonaia's autopsy, his consciousness returned to his body. He startled the medical examiners and they rushed him to surgery. Three days later, despite his severe injuries, he was able to tell them of the crying infant.

A subsequent examination of the infant revealed the broken hip, which not only validated Rodonaia's near-death experience, but also validated the survival of his consciousness *outside* of his physical body. He returned from his near-death experience a completely changed man and devoted the rest of his life to God, serving as a minister.

These two NDEs appear to corroborate Dr. Alexander's experience of the survival of consciousness outside of the physical body. The number of medically documented near-death experiences continues to grow. At this point, there are far too many on record for anyone to continue to believe that consciousness dies when the brain stops functioning.

The consciousness of both Harry Hone and George Rodonaia during their NDEs had to have remained intact and functioning outside their body, giving both men privileged information in the spiritual realm, which was later corroborated in the material world. Harry learned about the whereabouts of his long-lost sister and George Rodonaia discovered the infant with the broken hip.

As a grieving mother, it was exactly the type of reassurance I needed in order to understand that my son's soul or consciousness continued to survive. This validated the ongoing contact I continued to have with him. Even today, eleven years after my son's death, I am still able to experience different levels of consciousness apart from my own. It is believed that altering brain wave function and raising the vibration of the pineal gland stimulate the release of DMT.

If this is true, does the amount of DMT released by the pineal gland have a direct correlation with the type of spiritual event that follows? Are higher consciousness experiences, insight, enlightenment, precognition, clairvoyance, out of body experiences (OBE) and NDEs dependent on the amount of DMT flooding our brains?

Good Vibrations

George Rodonaia was attacked by the KGB and pronounced dead. Harry Hone temporarily died of cardiac arrest. Dr. Eben Alexander was in a coma with no functioning neocortex, and I experienced the death of a child. Did each of us experience consciousness separate and apart from the body: the three men as they separated from their physical bodies and connected with the consciousness of other individuals, and I in my state of grief as I connected with the consciousness of my son?

Could my experience have fired up the booster rocket but their experiences hit the "go" button? During the pain and stress of my grief, I noticed that the intensity of my vibration or energy level was greatly increased. I had a single-minded desire to connect with Spirit. Could the combination of these two occurrences have resulted in my ability to hear my son, feel his touch and presence, see Spirit, and interact with animals in unusual ways? Did it give me the ability to see and interact with orbs and have a number of other ongoing transpersonal experiences?

After reading Dr. Strassman's research, I believe the vibration I felt in my body was similar to the vibration the doctor's volunteers experienced when injected with DMT. Is it possible that DMT was released as a result of the stress from my loss? And is it possible that DMT had provided the environment or created the opportunity for one spiritual event after another?

I also considered the possibility that the vibration I experienced had "tuned me in" to a specific frequency that connected me to my son's consciousness. This would be similar to adjusting the dial on a radio to tune in the frequency band of a certain station. It may also explain why spiritual experiences with massive amounts of DMT, like those of Rodonaia, Hone and Dr. Alexander reached different, possibly higher frequencies on the spiritual spectrum.

When my vibration increased, I noticed that the appearance of orbs and my ability to see and feel their presence increased. In addition, I've noticed over the years that whenever I consciously raised my vibration through joy and excitement, my ability to connect with Spirit and consciousness outside my own existence increased. I could physically feel my heart leap and experience a surge of excitement at the thought of connecting with Spirit. I could then feel this heightened energy coursing through my body as I called out to Spirit either verbally or telepathically.

Was the appearance of orbs purely coincidental or a response to my vibration or frequency at the time? The number of instances in which this happened seemed far more than merely anecdotal. In my opinion, they were responding to both my telepathic and verbal call and appearing in order to be photographed.

If this were the case, then orbs possessed some form of consciousness and an ability to connect with my own. Was I generating a particular wave pattern, frequency or vibration in my brain that enabled me to communicate with consciousness outside my body?

Traditional Hindu customs identify a specific point of the human body responsible for spiritual experiences that coincidentally aligns with the location of the pineal gland. I mentioned earlier that Descartes identified the pineal gland as "the seat of the soul." Were they onto something that Western Science is just beginning to acknowledge?

Could the pineal gland have a dual role: acting as both a homing beacon and transmitter for the Divine? We all possess this tiny gland. Although millions of people around the world are photographing orbs, some are unsuccessful. I've noticed that many who have the ability to "call them in" are also open to the presence of Spirit and believe in the survival of consciousness.

Could these beliefs or, more importantly, the feelings these beliefs generate, have a direct effect on our pineal gland and our ability to connect with the Divine?

The pineal gland is part of our basic human equipment. Is it possible that DMT could be the Spirit Molecule, assuring our everlasting connection to God and our reconnection to the Divine at the moment of death or during stressful life events?

CHAPTER SEVEN

"There are two ways of spreading the light:
To be the candle or the mirror that reflects it."

~ Edith Wharton

Near-Death Experience and Orbs

Dr. Alexander is not the first person to see an orb or brilliant ball of light during a near-death experience. Many people who have shared their NDE stories describe encounters with guides and angels that have manifested from a ball of light. Some even describe their own consciousness or soul as a ball of light.

Raymond

Dr. Raymond Moody is the leading authority on the near-death experience. He is a bestselling author of twelve books on the subject, including *Life After Life: The Investigation of a Phenomenon—Survival of Bodily Death*, (with a foreword by the late Dr. Elisabeth Kübler-Ross, a world expert on death and dying), which has sold over 13 million copies worldwide.[57]

In his book, he investigates more than one hundred case studies of people who experience "clinical death" and were subsequently revived. According to his interviews with people who have had NDEs, Moody says, "Furthermore, despite its lack of perceptibility to people in physical bodies, all who have experienced it are in agreement that the spiritual body is nonetheless something, impossible to describe though it may be. It is agreed that the spiritual body has a form or shape (sometimes globular or an amorphous cloud, but also sometimes essentially the same shape as the physical body.")[58]

The following are excerpts from individual accounts of NDEs in *Life After Life*, which appear to be describing the characteristics of orbs:

> When my heart stopped beating…I felt like I was a round ball and almost maybe like I might have been a little sphere—like a BB—on the inside of this round ball…[59]

> I could feel something, some kind of a—like a capsule, or something, like a clear form. I couldn't really see it; it was like it was transparent, but not really. It was like I was just there—an energy, maybe, sort of like just a little ball of energy…[60]

> My being or myself or my spirit, or whatever you would like to label it—I could sort of feel it rise out of me, out through my head. And it wasn't anything that hurt, it was just sort of like lifting and it being above me…[My "being"] felt as if it had density to it, almost, but not a physical density-kind of like, I don't know, waves or something, I guess:

> Nothing really physical, almost as if it were charged, if you'd like to call it that. But it felt as if it had something to it…It was small, and it felt as if it were sort of circular, with no rigid outlines to it. You could liken it to a cloud… It almost seemed as if it were in its own encasement…[61]

Dr. Moody's case studies echo the description of the orbs we have seen in photographs, as does Dr. Tony Cicoria's experience.

Tony

During the August 2012 National Conference for the International Association of Near-death Studies (IANDS), I had the opportunity to listen to keynote speaker, Dr. Tony Cicoria. Tony is an orthopedic surgeon and in 1994, at the age of forty-two, he was struck by lightning while standing next to a telephone booth during a storm. The strike knocked Tony to the ground, stopping his heart. He recalled seeing his own body surrounded by a bluish-white light. A woman standing near him, who happened to be an intensive care nurse, began CPR in a desperate attempt to save his life.

But Tony had already left his body. He was dead.

Photo 82 (left). An orb touches Dr. Cicoria's head when he says he felt nudged to play the piano. Photo 83 (right). An orb appears above Dr. Cicoria after playing a song he composed on the piano after his NDE. © Virginia Hummel

With cool detachment, he watched the event unfold and then turned away to climb the stairs nearby. As he did so, he noticed that his legs began to disappear as he climbed. He said he felt himself became a "ball of bluish white light." The ball was approximately three feet in diameter and then began to shrink. He felt an enormous sense of peace and well-being. Suddenly, he found himself back in his body revived by the CPR. He felt pain and anger and cried out, "Please don't make me come back."

After his NDE, Tony began to have an insatiable desire to hear classical piano music. He was compelled to learn to play the piano and compose the piece of music he'd heard during his NDE that now played relentlessly in his head. He said if he didn't practice the piano every day the song played over and over in his head until he did.

During Tony's keynote speech, I took two photos of him. Photo 82 was taken at the exact moment he mentioned that the song plays over and over in his head. Notice the orb attached to Tony's head. If orbs are connected to the human soul or consciousness, it is possible that Tony has a guide who is encouraging him to compose this music?

The bluish orb in Photo 83 was taken just after Tony finished playing the composition he'd written after his NDE on the piano. He had returned to the stage during a standing ovation. Tony said, "It took a million volts of energy to get me to make that leap of faith."

Carter

Author and researcher P.M.H. Atwater shares the near-death experience of Carter Mills in *Beyond the Light*.[62] While at work, a massive load of compressed cardboard that Mills was loading slipped out of control, slamming him against a steel pole. During his NDE, Mills describes himself as a ball of light. He is taken by angels to an audience with Jesus.

> Instantly Mills's whole life began to play out, starting at birth. He relived being a tiny spark of light traveling to Earth as soon as egg and sperm met and entering his mother's womb. In mere seconds, he had to choose hair color and eyes out of the genetic material available to him and any genes that might give him the body he would need.
>
> He bypassed the gene for club footedness, and then watched from a soul's perspective as cells subdivided. He could hear his parents whenever they spoke and feel their emotions, but any knowledge of his past lives dissolved.
>
> Jesus and the angels disintegrated into a giant sphere of light once Carter no longer needed their shape or form to put him at ease. As the sphere grew it absorbed him, infused him with the ecstasy of unconditional love…He zoomed back to his

mangled remains as a ball of all-knowing light and crashed into his solar plexus with such force it jolted his body to action.

Rachel

The following story is taken from Dr. Long's website NDERF.org (Near-Death Experience Research Foundation). After being hit by a car, Rachel describes "popping" out of her body and becoming a golden orb.

> I was hit by a car as a pedestrian. At the moment of being hit, it became surreal. I knew as the car hit my left leg that it was happening but everything began happening in slow motion. After hitting the windshield, I was thrown sixty-five feet and remember flying through the air. As I hit the pavement and started sliding, I felt I should leave my body.
>
> When my body came to a stop after sliding on the pavement, I "popped" out of the body and continued upward beyond my control but felt the body was "no good" and accepted that I was "moving on." After experiencing a period of time that I was in complete darkness and only felt myself being pulled through buoyant barriers, I came upon an opening. I then was greeted by five to ten golden "orbs" which I felt I knew and it was like a "reunion."
>
> It was the most joy and ecstasy I had ever felt when they greeted me. I knew them within. One orb approached me and showed me that I was the same, and when it combined with me, I realized that I was also a golden orb. I was then pulled back and even more quickly than I had gotten to this other world, I was back in my body.[63]

As a mother whose child has died in a motorcycle accident, my one hope was that Christopher didn't suffer. I had heard stories how we just pop out of our body at the time of death, but I didn't really know for sure if they were true. I saw the accident scene photos and the metal pole he impacted before landing in a ditch.

As parents, we would do anything to protect our children, even take their pain if possible. I wasn't there that night to protect him or hold him as he took his last breath. My mind can only imagine the pain and suffering my child must have felt on impact and the moments afterward.

Yet Rachel's story and many others like it have lifted a great weight off my shoulders knowing at the time of impact it was possible they just "popped" out of their physical body and continued living, consciousness and all. Not only were they still alive, albeit in a different form, they were loved and cared for by beings on the other side, many of which were friends and family who had also crossed over. If that was the case, then it was possible that my son also "popped" out of his body and was being loved and cared for on the other side too.

Claude Swanson, PhD, author of *The Synchronized Universe Series* states that:

> In the out of body experience (OBE), the astral body, or sometimes the mental body is used as a vehicle. A self-contained subtle energy field, which we usually perceive as an orb, is created into which consciousness is placed, and can travel while the physical body remains behind.[64]

> This may explain why orbs are sometimes seen at death, and are considered to contain the consciousness after-death. This is the beginning of a scientific understanding of the "soul."[65]

It was intriguing to me that a physicist was able to embrace the idea that consciousness could exist outside the physical body when the majority of the scientific community believed otherwise.

"Are orbs are connected to the afterlife?" I asked.

Swanson answered, "Nurses and hospice workers who are present at time of death have reported in many cases an orb leaving the body."

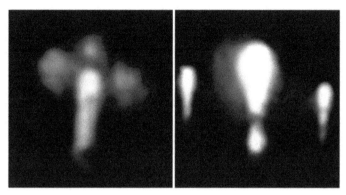

Photo 84 (left), Photo 85 (right) © Naomi Fugiwara. Beings of light.

David

I recently read Eben Alexander's new book, *The Map of Heaven: How Science, Religion, and Ordinary People Are Proving the Afterlife* and discovered the following story from David Palmer. It was so compelling that I immediately contacted David for an interview. He shares the last few emotional moments with his father:

> My father had been in hospice for nearly two weeks after suffering a series of strokes in August of 1999. Our family had finally made the difficult decision to let him go from his unresponsive state. My three siblings and I remained on a constant vigil in the hospital the last few days before he crossed, so that he was never alone.
>
> At four o'clock AM, dad's breathing slowed and signaled the end was near. We sat in his darkened room, lit only by a small night-light attached to the wall near the bathroom. There was no equipment or monitors with lights in the room, which was located on the sixth or seventh floor of the hospital. There wasn't any other ambient light, not even from the window.

Seated in a chair a foot from his bedside, I stared at my father. He was facing me as he took his last breath. As I began to rise from my chair, I noticed what appeared to be a three-eighths inch to one half-inch piece of white thread or something similar that had settled on my dad's temple. I suddenly thought, *the nerve of that piece of thread to land right there! Where in the heck did it come from?*

I wanted to flick it away. I shouldn't have been able to see a tiny thread or piece of lint on my father's temple because of the darkened room. While I could see the outline of his eyes and hair, it was so dark that if I hadn't known him, I wouldn't have been able to distinguish the color of his skin.

Dumbfounded, I stared at the thread and wondered where it came from and why it appeared illuminated. I glanced up and searched the ceiling and room for another light source but found none. As I stared at the thread, it almost looked as if it were trying to stretch, similar to the movement of butterfly wing emerging from a cocoon. This little thread appeared to have movement in it, and for a second, I wondered if a bug had landed on my dad's head. Now, I'm almost mad and thinking, *Come on! He just died and something landed on his head!*

Suddenly, I noticed a little brightness coming from underneath the thread. At this point, I'm completely mesmerized, but I couldn't make sense of what I was seeing and rubbed my eyes to refocus. Tiny little rays of sparkling light begin to appear. As they grew, an iridescent sky-blue color appeared with the sparkling rays.

It may have been five or ten seconds later that a little blue orb slowly emerged from my dad's temple. Once free, it rested for a moment on dad's skin, balanced on the rays of sparkling light that acted like legs. Then it slowly rose a foot or two above his head, hovered for a few seconds, then purposefully moved off toward the southwest corner of the hospital room.

Oddly, it happened to be in the same direction as his childhood home located a block away. I turned to follow it and watched the little blue orb rise up and disappear into the ceiling.

Stunned, I turned back towards my siblings at the foot of his bed and stared at the silhouette of my younger sister, Jackie. I fully expected someone to say something, but no one did.

"Did something just happen here?" I asked, not wanting to put words in their mouths.

Jackie replied, "You mean that light that just came out of the side of dad's head and floated away?"

She had seen it too, but my older brother and sister who were standing behind my little sister at the time had not.

Jackie says, "I only saw very bright, sparkling, bluish-green lights dancing on the side of dad's head, twinkling. It makes me smile whenever I think of it. They seemed to stay there, dancing around by his temple. He was a very dear, funny man, very smart, and a bit sarcastic. I felt he was saying goodbye by twinkling at me—I was his baby and looked a lot like him.

David and his sister each received a wonderful gift that night, one in the form of an iridescent, sky-blue orb with sparkling rays and the other as bright sparkling bluish-green lights. Could the orb and sparkling lights that emerged from their father's head have been his soul or consciousness? The little sky-blue orb appeared to have acted with intention as it rested, rose, hovered and headed off in a specific direction after it emerged from his father's temple.

David's description of the thread that appeared on his father's temple reminded me of Alan's story in Chapter Three where Alan describes "'something white' like *seeing a piece of fur from my ginger and white cat* but, as I took a step forward, the 'something white' suddenly transformed into a spinning circle of light."

Is it possible that both of these experiences are describing the same thing? Could what David referred to as a thread that transformed into an orb, and what Alan referred to as a piece of fur which transformed into a circle of light be connected to the human soul?

Their experiences validated my research, experience and intuitive *knowing* that orbs are connected to the human soul or consciousness. Many near-death experiencers have described their "soul" as a ball of light or orb. They have also referred to others as a spark, orb, or being of light during their journey to the other side.

These descriptions seem to mimic the characteristics of orbs that we see in digital photography and help to validate my theory about orbs and their connection to the human soul. Could David's orb be the final piece of the puzzle needed to prove that consciousness survives death and is able to manifest as an orb?

CHAPTER EIGHT

"Bright balls of luminous light with tails moved clockwise in a circle
like a miniature Ferris wheel."

~Erica McKenzie, RN

Seeing Orbs After NDEs

Many who have experienced near-death are vastly transformed by the
event. They may seem supercharged, as if they've been plugged into
the Source once again. Sometimes the change is so drastic they are
unable to continue the life they had before their NDE. They seek out a
new life aligned with their authentic self, memories and feelings from
the other side.

Erica

Because of their heightened vibrational level, one of the possible after-
effects of a near-death experience is the ability to see orbs without the
aid of a camera. Erica McKenzie is a registered nurse and hospice
worker who had experienced the ultimate NDE in 2002. She talked
with God. Her book, *Dying to Fit In,* recounts her visit to Heaven, her
lengthy discussion with God, and the messages He has asked her to
deliver.[66]

Although Erica had always believed in God and was a member of
the Lutheran Church, she returned from her NDE with the realization

that a person's religious affiliation was not important. God was the same God for all people. The connection with Him was most important. She also returned with the ability to deliver divine messages to people to aid in their healing and growth. She says it is important to note that not everyone is ready to hear these messages, as they require the willingness to do the inner work to effect the change.

Erica contacted me through my Orb Whisperer website and insisted that we speak. Shortly after, I interviewed Erica over the phone for the first time. Her NDE and the story leading up to it kept me on the edge of my seat for three hours. I knew I was in the presence of someone who had experienced something very special. I could feel it.

After my conversation with Erica, despite the fifteen hundred mile distance between us, I vibrated at such a high rate and intensity I could barely talk. During the following twenty-four hours, I was physically exhausted from interacting with Erica and her stepped up vibrational rate caused by her near-death experience.

One of the many gifts Erica received that especially thrilled me was her ability to see orbs. Erica says:

> I started to clearly see orbs in May of 2012 when I was on a flight home from Orlando to Kansas City. In the clouds outside the window, a swirling pattern formed. It looked to be some sort of vortex. Bright balls of luminous light with tails moved clockwise in a circle like a miniature Ferris wheel. There were too many to count.

> At Virginia's suggestion, I recently read *Proof of Heaven* and Dr. Alexander describes the same balls of light with tails during his NDE that I can see playing in the clouds.

> After contacting Virginia to ask her about them, she encouraged me to use my gifts from my NDE to find out more about them by asking God and the orbs direct questions. God said that once we cross over, souls have the choice to visit Earth or stay in Heaven. What I had seen

outside the airplane window were the balls of light or "orbs" that were visiting Earth.

Also, I walk about six to eight miles every day and I have been doing this for several months now. About two weeks ago, I was able to see the orbs while I was walking. They actually stayed with me through the entire walk. They all have faces, but I have not been able to focus well enough yet to be able to identify the faces. There are always multiple orbs present and they seem to travel together. I noticed that orbs appear near power lines and I have wondered if they somehow get energy from the electricity or if it helps them to be able to appear.

In February of 2013, I called Virginia during my morning walk and I began to describe the orbs to her. She asked me to stop walking, reach out, and call them closer. They swarmed around my fingertips just out of reach. They were the size of golf balls and clear with a bit of a shimmer.

Just beyond them hovered a brilliant ball of light with a tail, different from the small orbs at my fingertips. I got the distinct impression that it was supervising the smaller ones, much like a babysitter. Suddenly, off to my right was something completely different. A squiggle! It had a thin dark outline, the viscosity of mercury and moved much like a snake.

Soon I discovered a tennis ball sized orb with a dark ring and glowing center who I intuitively knew as my angelic guide. He always appears as I walk. On a recent trip to Disneyworld with my family, I was reading a book Virginia had given me, *The Power of Intention,* by Wayne Dyer.

At certain points, minuscule orbs would congregate on the page I was reading. I took particular care to pay attention to the words they were swarming around. My guide also appeared and for the first time came close to me, shrank in size and landed on the page. I knew he was telling me to pay attention to the message delivered through Wayne.

Today on my walk, I found myself communicating with the many orbs that came to me. I thought, *you are all getting so much bigger than I have seen you before.* I told them I would like to understand more about them and hoped to see them fully manifest into a human form. I told them I would love to be able to know their names and purpose with me. I went on to tell them I would love to know and see everything. I said aloud to God, "If it is your will and you feel I am ready, I ask to see these orbs and Spirits more clearly and who they are revealed to me."

Then I looked up and watched all of the different orbs coming toward me. I delighted in their presence as I studied them. Suddenly, an orb in the most beautiful pearl white and enveloping energy appeared at my distant upper right. She was the size of a basketball. She floated gracefully and slowly, stopped for a brief moment, and then moved to my left directly in front of me.

As I watched in awe, it materialized into a divinely beautiful woman. She was my height but I could only see her figure from the waist up. Her body was positioned in a side profile, but her face was turned directly toward me. She wore white clothes like in the time of Jesus and a covering on her head that draped down past her shoulders. Her face was a silhouette in white pearl. She was not like the other orbs. I was mesmerized and humbled by her appearance.

Most of the orbs I see with faces inside them are outlined in soft black. She was completely different. I have noticed that each orb is as unique as the people are on Earth. Even though some orbs appear to look similar, the closer they get to me, the easier it is to see that all their faces are different.

Erica has continued to develop her relationship with these beautiful balls of light or orbs. Almost daily she shares a new experience with me by text or phone. The insight she has revealed has been invaluable in our ongoing quest to discover new information about the meaning and intention of these magnificent beings of light.

She has helped me to validate my research and experiences with orbs—that they are indeed real and can be a visual manifestation of consciousness with which we can communicate. Erica's ability to see faces inside orbs validated the appearance of faces that many are discovering in orb photos.

Muriel

Muriel Lowndes emailed me after she visited my website, and described her experience with orbs. Muriel says:

> I am an old lady of eighty-eight years. I live in Scotland and have seen orbs in my bedroom for the past six years. Since I moved to a new house a year ago, I see them every night in bed either before I go to sleep or before daybreak. Usually three orbs appear; the largest is the size of a beach ball while the smallest is tennis ball sized.
>
> They are a dark blackish color with a golden sheen and light center. They dance around the wall and respond when I speak to them. I now ask one to come into my hand, which it does, and then I put my hand on my heart and it disappears into my heart.
>
> I feel they are messengers and they bring me great comfort and soothe away any troubles I may have. I do some healing work when I am able and think perhaps they give me energy for that.

After I read Muriel's email, I replied and asked if she would allow me to use her story in my book. In the meantime, I tentatively placed her story near my own story related later in the book about the orb that had appeared on my chest and had allowed me to examine it. Both of us described details that are not seen in photographs.

As I started to work on this section of the book relating stories about NDEs and orbs, I had a sudden urge to move her story from that later chapter to this one. Somehow, I knew that Muriel had an NDE, even though she hadn't mentioned this in her email.

In my Inbox the following morning was a reply email from Muriel confirming my intuition. The rest of her story included her NDE as a child. She had also experienced something else that was unusual. Muriel has the gift of healing hands.

> My healing ability began seven years ago, after I had lost the power in my right hand. When the power came back I felt an enormous amount of energy in that hand and people responded so positively in physical and mental ways when I used that hand for gentle massage.
>
> It was about this time that I first saw the orbs and I have been privileged to help many people over these years with what I call my healing hand, although the power is not mine. It is a gift and gives me great joy. It feels as if so many of my experiences have led to where I am today and for me the orbs have become like friends. It is a joy to go to bed at night knowing I will most likely see them.

Corroborating an Orb Experience

While attending the August 2012 National IANDS Conference, I had the opportunity to listen to Dr. Alexander's keynote presentation, "Consciousness and the NDE: Beyond 2012." At one point, he seemed visibly moved as he spoke of "The Girl on the Butterfly Wing." I could feel his outpouring of heartfelt emotion the moment he realized it had been Betsy, his birth sister, who had accompanied him on his near-death journey.

Physically and intuitively, I could feel an energy or consciousness present in the room and I was compelled to reach for my camera. I *knew* his sister was here with him. I snapped one picture of the stage and screen the moment he revealed the photograph of his guardian angel, Betsy.

Betsy was glorious—radiant, as she stood in the warm glow of a California sunset with her golden-brown locks and the sparkle of divine light in her blue eyes. There were audible gasps from the audience as they recognized with clarity the truth behind this picture and the powerful message it held for all of us.

The photo on my camera flashed before my eyes, a brief, shining glimpse of the truth we all seek. There were several wispy orbs in Photo 86, but one especially bright orb next to the large photograph of his birth sister.

In all the years of photographing orbs, I have never attempted to identify the light beings in the photos. Although I can feel their energy, I prefer to allow the beholder of the photograph to use their own experience and intuition as a guide to the identity of the specific orbs they capture.

This particular photograph is an exception. Because I felt such a strong energy present in the room with us before and after Dr. Alexander revealed the identity of "The Girl on the Butterfly Wing," and because of the position of the bright orb, I intuitively knew the instant it flashed on my camera screen, that I had captured his beautiful sister in her full magnificence as a spark of divine light.

The moment was so powerful for me that it brought tears to my eyes. What are the odds that I would capture a brilliant ball of light next to "Betsy's" photo with one shot?

When the presentation ended, I stood just outside the lecture hall talking about the photo. Nola Davis, CEO of a health care corporation and tireless advocate for the education of seniors regarding the spiritual aspects of death, overheard my conversation and stepped forward. Nola is the co-author of *Live From the Other Side*, which combines the areas of spirituality, hospice, bereavement, personal growth and metaphysics.[67] She is also an intuitive.

Photo 86 © Virginia Hummel. An orb appears near the right side of the screen in the exact moment Alexander reveals his deceased sister as "the girl on the butterfly wing."

Nola said she watched a beautiful bluish-white light follow Dr. Alexander onto the stage and was surprised that it formed a full apparition of a lovely woman standing just behind his shoulder. She jotted down her description in a journal and noted that the woman was present during his lecture. As Dr. Alexander spoke from his heart, she moved closer to him on his right side. When he ventured into his scientific mode, she stepped away.

At one point, Nola said she looked up and second-guessed what she was seeing and experiencing as the woman stood behind Alexander. Suddenly the woman captured Nola's gaze and she heard her say telepathically, "You stick to what you know..." which meant to Nola that she was not to doubt what she was seeing or experiencing. Then Nola telepathically said, "Thank you for the gift."

Nola was stunned when Dr. Alexander revealed Betsy's photograph on the screen; it was the same woman she had seen standing behind him on the stage. Later, Dr. Alexander confirmed that he too felt his sister's presence with him during his lecture, as he had during past lectures on his near-death experience.

Photo 87 (left). Bill Guggenheim & Eben Alexander 2014 IANDS Conference. Photo 88 (right). Alexander with an orb at his back. © Virginia Hummel.

Photo 89 © Virginia Hummel. Bill Guggenheim at the 2013 IANDS Conf. Orb appears as he reminisces about his friend.

Nola's description of Betsy as a bluish-white light validated my photo of the bluish-white orb next to Betsy's picture. I don't believe it is a coincidence that Nola saw Betsy behind Alexander while I felt Betsy's presence and was urged to pick up my camera. (See Photo 88 for example)

Claude Swanson, Ph.D., author of *Life Force, The Scientific Basis: Breakthrough Physics of Energy medicine, Healing, Chi and Quantum Consciousness* says, "Many phenomena are seen by 'sensitives' or clairvoyants, even though they do not appear on photographic film…most photographs taken reveal only a spot of light, an orb."[68]

Photo 87 of Dr. Alexander and Bill Guggenheim was taken during the 2014 IANDS Conference and shows a large blue orb overhead along with several smaller white ones. It is interesting to note that a second large blue orb was captured in Photo 89 during Bill's presentation. Bill had just mentioned his good friend Elizabeth Kübler Ross. More often than not, if I pay attention, I discover that Spirit is alive, well, and participating in our lives if we are open to the signs.

John

While attending a spiritual self-help Conference in November 2011, I had the opportunity to hear renowned psychic medium John Holland speak. He had pulled a woman to the front of the stage and began talking about her deceased father. The man was so insistent to talk to his daughter through John, he had to tell the man repeatedly to wait until he had finished having a conversation with his daughter.

We all laughed at the invisible antics happening on stage. What I found so interesting was the moment John said, "Okay, you can come on in and talk now," I snapped a photo of an orb near the woman. You may even be able to see John's left arm motioning the man into the conversation. (Photo 90)

John also did some wonderfully accurate readings for people as the one of the Keynote speakers at the International Conference on After-Death Communication. During a reading for a woman who had lost her mother a decade before, John was able to connect with the mother.

Photo 91 shows a large orb above the woman's head. I along with several people could see a woman's face inside it. We could see short curly hair and a three-quarter profile of a woman in the orb in Photos 92 and 93, although the lady having the reading was not able to see a face in the orb.

Photo 90 © Virginia Hummel. An orb appears as Holland motions for a loved one to join their conversation.

Photo 91 (left). Holland connects with the standing woman's deceased mom. Photo 92 (upper right). A face of a woman appears in the orb. Photo 93 (lower right) Color contrast. ©Virginia Hummel.

Barbara

At another conference, I met Barbara Stone Bakstad. We had just come from James Van Praggh's session where my son came through in a reading. When that session ended, Barbara and I walked together into John Holland's session. Barb had recently lost her son David and had hoped to hear from him through James.

As we sat down in John's session and waited for it to begin, I began to pray silently for her to have a reading with David. I knew how healing it could be and felt she needed it.

Barb received the second reading of the session from John. He pointed to the area where we were sitting and said, "I have a little boy here who drowned." Barb's sister stood up and said, "Yes, that's Adam. He was two and a half years old. He's my sister's son."

Photo 94 © Virginia Hummel. John Holland the moment he says, "I have your two boys here with me." (See arrows)

There was a collective gasp in the auditorium as our hearts went out to Adam and his mother. John proceeded to talk with Barb and then said, "I have a second male energy here that also drowned. Do you know who I am talking about?" The person John referred to was Barb's twenty-one-year-old son David who had recently died. After a short discussion with Barbara, John said, "I have your two boys with me on stage." I snapped Photo 94 at that very moment. Notice the two orbs with John to his left.

John tends to use humor as a wonderful way to shift the energy in the room as the circumstances surrounding the death of a loved one during a reading can be very emotional. John suddenly said, "There's a parrot sitting on my shoulder. Do you know anything about this?"

Barb blurted out, "The parrot drowned too!"

The audience laughed at the irony of the situation if only as a relief from tragic circumstances Barbara experienced. A storm had blown its cage over and the parrot escaped, only to be swept into the water.

Over the last few years as I have gotten to know Barb, I have discovered her wonderful sense of humor. Despite her losses, she uses it to help her find balance in her grief journey. We all needed some levity after learning she had lost two boys and we were grateful she was to be able to make a joke of the poor parrot's demise to lighten the energy in the room.

As for these photographs, I find the timing and appearance of these orbs more than coincidental. Could the balls of light seen in digital photos, and sometimes by the human eye, be visual proof of life after death? Are we experiencing the presence of consciousness outside our bodies as an orb? The beauty and truth of these stories give us the opportunity to make the leap and "get it" while we are here in this lifetime. Imagine how much comfort we all might have if we knew without a doubt, that death was just a momentary transition.

These deeply moving examples from Spirit through orb encounters and NDEs continue to grow in number around the world. We must ask ourselves how much more proof we need before we step from our willful ignorance, and acknowledge that consciousness and life continues after the moment of metamorphosis we call death.

Each of us has the opportunity to choose our "aha" moment. Those who have chosen to step into the light and embrace the idea that consciousness survives death are discovering they are not only experiencing life on multi-dimensional levels; they are also experiencing the miracle of connection to their loved ones who have transitioned before them. This extraordinary connection aids in their grief healing.

CHAPTER NINE

"Ask and it is given to you; seek and you will find;
knock and the door shall be opened for you."

~ Matthew 7:7

The Urge to Know

Although countless near-death experiencers know for sure that there is life after death, many of us still wonder if there is something more. Imagine for a moment that death isn't an ending but a metamorphosis, a shedding of our physical body to reveal our authentic self, a shift to our natural state of being that is so comforting and real, once we have experienced it, we can no longer envision ourselves in any other form.

What if we could see this state of being? What if there was a way to see the other side of death, a manifestation of our authentic self, our soul, or consciousness energy? What an incredible thought! Imagine the implications of finally knowing without a doubt that we are more than just our physical body and that we really do live on after-death.

Imagine the comfort of realizing that our loved ones who have crossed before us are still safe and very much "alive." They have only made the shift from a physical to a spiritual state, like a caterpillar to a butterfly. Life doesn't end with our physical death, but continues on eternally in a different state of being. David Palmer's experience with the tiny orb emerging from his father's temple and the appearance of

Betsy as an orb during Dr. Alexander's NDE has given us beautifully documented examples of this. They both had a unique experience, and a profound awakening and healing through the miracle of Spirit.

Awakenings come in many forms, but are most commonly triggered by some sort of sudden emotional or physical trauma. Dr. Stanislav Grof, author of *The Adventure of Self Discovery: Dimensions of Consciousness and New Perspectives in Psychotherapy and Inner Exploration* writes:

> Experiences of encounters with guides, teachers, and protectors from the spiritual world belong to the most valuable and rewarding phenomena of the transpersonal domain...Sometimes they appear quite spontaneous at a certain state of the spiritual development of an individual; other times they suddenly emerge during an inner crisis, responding for an urgent call for help.[69]

In the book, *A Soul's Journey,* author Peter Richelieu also writes about how our urge to know more about life on the spiritual plane develops after a crisis. He writes:

> It required some great tragedy, such as the death of his well-loved brother Charles, to make him clamor for light, for occult knowledge; there had to be a crisis for through this, the urge to know is born.[70]

My own "urge to know" came in February 2006 when my youngest son Christopher died in a motorcycle accident. The loss of a child is one of the most painful and profound emotional experiences we can have. We question ourselves and our beliefs. We question almost everything about our life and we ask why. Why did it happen to us? What did we do wrong?

I'd heard that with tragedy came the opportunity for spiritual growth. I knew through reading and experience that I was the creator of my reality. Why wasn't I also the creator of my experience with death as well? I had the choice to create grace or despair. I chose grace because for me there was no other option.

How else could I make sense of all the harsh realities in the world: the wars and starvation, cruelty, utter inhumanity and indifference— even the loneliness, pain and heartache of my own experiences? There had to be a reason for all of this. Life had to have a greater purpose. Surely there was a larger picture. Otherwise, life seemed too inhumane. Why would anyone want to participate?

William Peters, MFT, M.Ed., is the founder of the *Shared Crossings Project*[71] in Santa Barbara, California. He suffered an NDE during a high-speed skiing accident at the age of seventeen. During our interview, William said:

> I remember being in the tube or tunnel and I realized I had been here before hundreds if not thousands of times. There was a real weightiness to that realization in a certain way because human lives have a purpose and a lot of them are quite painful. I have come to learn that being on Earth is like school.
>
> You check into a school with an intention and a set of objectives for a higher cause to evolve the soul. It wasn't just for my benefit or one soul, but for the benefit of all beings. These are work missions. It's not to say there's not joy in human life, there is, but the real intention, as I see it, is that we come with specific objectives.

The death of my son created a black hole too frightening to comprehend. The thought of his absence, his total obliteration was so overwhelming, the pain threatened to consume me. I knew I wasn't going to survive it unless I clung to the knowledge and belief I had possessed since childhood that there was indeed a bigger picture. I believe there has to be a reason and meaning to everything we experience as a human.

Therefore, I believe my son's death happened for a reason. With that in mind, I was determined to find that reason. The Carmelite nuns say my son was neither lost nor dead, but instead, "at a different address." If this were true, I just needed to find his address. Then I could communicate with him, and with his help, I would find some answers. In the process, I could not only help myself; I could also help others who were going through the same experience.

It was a hell of a challenge but I chose to stand in grace, to honor my son by being the best I could be, to have unwavering faith in my belief that life is eternal. I could have let this event destroy me, but instead I let it inspire me. I chose to grasp the opportunity to awaken and embrace the growth presented by this tragedy.

Louis LaGrand, Ph.D. is one of the world's leading grief counselors and author of several books including *Love Lives On: Learning from the Extraordinary Encounters of the Bereaved.* He says that the pivotal question all mourners face is: "Will I be loss oriented or restoration oriented? Will you make sorrow your way of life or will you choose a path to peace?"[72]

Attending Dr. LaGrand's workshop in 2011 was a privilege. He is kind, compassionate, funny and an exceedingly bright light who brilliantly shifts the dark energy of mourning the loss of a loved one into an event that we are able to manage and even overcome. It was a huge relief to know that he validated the way I chose to move forward and be restoration oriented after the loss of my son despite how others felt. Moving forward that way brought me peace.

It is interesting to note that the Universe is right on track, regardless of what I experience, or how difficult the challenge. My life has been one synchronistic event after another. By focusing the direction of my thoughts and aligning myself with God, Source and I AM Presence, I allow the grace of all that is, to flow through me.

It is my job to encourage that grace to unfold with abundance, joy and miracles. When I stop that flow through fear or negative thinking, my experiences follow that train of thought. It has taken a lifetime to understand the degree of power and responsibility involved in creating every moment of my life, whether those moments are joyous or painful.

This doesn't mean that I didn't grieve the death of my child. I curled into the fetal position and wailed with the best of them. Although my spirit knew with unerring certainty that my son was fine, my heart was broken. Despite my emotional and physical pain, I felt compelled to stand in the light, to look up, not back, to cling hard and fast to my intuitive *knowing* that we are more than just a physical body.

Almost immediately after Chris's departure, I started to receive signs that he hadn't left after all. I had taught my son about life after death and had always believed there was more to life than what we could physically see.

Dr. Alexander's experience of meeting his birth sister during his NDE strongly suggests that my instincts of life beyond this third dimension were correct. It also meant there was a strong possibility that my son Christopher had survived in some other form.

Thoughts in Action

Many of us are unaware that our thoughts, words and actions can have a profound effect on each other, even those whom we haven't met. The following are examples of the effect of our interconnections.

In September of 2011, I met Patricia Alexander at a writer's conference in Phoenix, Arizona. We were instantly at ease with each other and felt as if we were old friends. We realized that we've known each other during many lifetimes and that we were both here to assist one another.

At the closing prayer of the conference, I could feel Spirit in the room. I captured a wonderful large moving blue white orb the size of a cantaloupe, near the producer of the conference and two of the guest editors. I had intended to send them the photo, but for some reason I never got around to doing so.

Patricia then decided that we should attend a spiritual self-help conference in November of 2011, also in Phoenix. It was the same producer. Patricia insisted that I not only attend the conference; I was also going to be her roommate. I couldn't tell her that I had absolutely no intention of doing either.

At the time, I had orbs on my mind, along with Wayne Dyer, who happened to be a presenter at this upcoming conference.[73] I had a feeling that he was connected to assisting me in moving the orb message forward.

A week before the conference I was shamed into buying a ticket. On the day I purchased my ticket, I suddenly got the overwhelming urge that I needed business cards and scrambled to make them. On Tuesday morning, forty-eight hours before my plane left for the conference, I got the overwhelming message that I needed an orb website.

Tilting my face toward Heaven I said, "You've got to be kidding me. I can't possibly do that in forty-eight hours!" I knew nothing about websites and I didn't have the funds or anyone available to build one for me on such short notice—especially one with a multiple photo layout and all the explanations.

It was no use arguing with God and Spirit. They demanded action. Patricia thought I was crazy and told me so. It was up to me, so I spent the next thirty plus hours over the following two days, learning about and building the beginning of my Orb Whisperer website.

Wayne Dyer had taken up residence in my head for the past six weeks and I knew that somehow, he was connected but I didn't know exactly how he would help me with my orb message.

Wayne

Friday evening in Phoenix, as we sat listening to Dr. Dyer's wonderful keynote speech, he mentioned orbs. I nearly fell off my chair. I could feel an energetic shift in the room and I reached for my camera. I managed to capture Photo 95 of Wayne surrounded by twenty orbs, many of which were blue. Photo 96 of Wayne Dyer with two large blue orbs was taken at another conference.

In 2012, I discovered what I believed to be a solid explanation for the orb color spectrum. I call it "The Newton Connection" after Michael Newton, Ph.D., author of *Journey of Souls: New Case Studies of Life between Lives.*[74] Newton, a hypnotherapist, has regressed clients into super states of consciousness to access their lives between lives.

Photo 95 © Virginia Hummel. Wayne Dyer with a room full of blue orbs.

Newton and his associates have regressed over seven thousand clients who were able to access their soul groups, guides and teachers. Within the groups, each individual soul radiated a different color, or variations of colors, suggesting their level of spiritual development. His clients' consensus was that souls who radiated a blue color were master teachers.

My intuition told me that the colors of orbs and the colors Newton's clients identified as souls were connected. If orbs were a manifestation of our soul or consciousness energy then wasn't it possible the blue orbs, captured during Wayne's Keynote speech, were souls representative of the blue master teacher energy?

Nonetheless, it was inspiring to see Wayne surrounded by these blue orbs. I cannot assume to know what color Wayne's soul would radiate, but after listening to him that particular night, I knew he was indeed a master teacher; his message was profound. It was obvious to me as I reviewed the photo that Wayne had some very powerful friends on the other side, helping him awaken and educate the audience in that room.

Photo 96 © Virginia Hummel. Wayne Dyer with blue orbs.

The following morning, I printed the photo of Wayne along with the orb photo I'd taken at a conference two months earlier, and set out to find the conference producer. Twice during the weekend, I tried to approach her: once she was unavailable and the other time she was nowhere to be found. It wasn't until the third time I tried to connect with her toward the end of the conference that it all fell beautifully into place. I unveiled the orb photo that included her and the two editors and then showed her Wayne's photo taken Friday evening.

My jaw dropped as I watched synchronicity in full bloom. She looked past me and called out to a woman across the foyer, "Have you Fed-Exed the package to Wayne yet?"

"No," she answered. "I was just walking out the door to take care of it."

The producer summoned her over and slipped my photo into the envelope bound for Wayne Dyer. I handed her my business card to include with it that Spirit insist I make.

On Monday morning, I awoke feeling super-charged with energy. I felt as if I were getting ready to be shot out into the universe! I was walking on air. Something was coming, but I didn't know what.

Orb ADC

In the early morning hours of Wednesday September 21, 2011, three days after the conference, I had my first ADC dream with orbs. The orb ADC dream was such an unexpected gift, I awoke in a state of complete joy and excitement. I was bubbling over from my encounter with these beautiful beings.

During the experience, I found myself in the living room of an unfamiliar house. Near the floor, I caught sight of a small translucent orb the size of a large marble. I blinked several times and stared at it until it dawned on me what I was viewing. Thrilled at finally being able to just "see" them without the aid of a camera and giggling with the curiosity and delight of a young child, I bent over with the full intention of clapping my hands together to pop this beautiful little bubble of silvery light.

Just before impact, it darted between my palms and hovered a few inches above my hands. It seemed to be glaring at me. I could feel the intensity of its disappointment that I would even consider hurting it after it had trusted me enough to appear. Instantly filled with remorse, I was disappointed in myself for attempting to pop this little being.

"I'm sorry. I don't know why I did that. I promise never to hurt you," I said aloud.

Suddenly another orb appeared, only larger. It was about the size of a small orange. My heart lifted and I was filled with all the wonder and delight of a child on Christmas morning. "Oh my God, I can really see them!" I cried out. "They are magnificent!"

This new orb floated around in the room, just out of reach. It was watching me—testing me to see if I understood the ramifications of having manifested here for me to see without a flash and a camera.

Intuitively I knew it was a major step, a breakthrough for both of us. I also knew that I must assume the full responsibility of stewardship and spokesperson for these beautiful beings.

The larger orb floated upward toward the ceiling. I then watched as the air above me began to swirl like a vortex. Suddenly the ceiling opened and hundreds of tiny orbs poured forth, surrounded by sparkles and covered in a plasma-like gel. Instinctively, I reached up and caught them in a huge pile in my arms. It was like a living, writhing mass of light-filled energy. I can't begin to describe the level of excitement and joy that enveloped my entire being. It was almost like being tickled to my soul. I called out to my family in the next room. "Oh my God, you're never going to believe this. They're everywhere!"

Photo 97 © Diana Davatgar. Diana in a cloud of orbs.

As I awoke that morning, I was filled with excitement. The ADC dream was astoundingly real and I retained the memory and feeling of holding the mass of tiny orbs. I bounced out of bed and called Patricia. I was vibrating at such a rate, it was that "swimming in champagne" feeling I've described before. The feeling was unnerving.

In retrospect, I realize this must have been what Dr. Rick Strassman meant when he said that nearly every one of the volunteers remarked about the vibrations brought on by the DMT (N, N-Dimethyltryptamine) mentioned in Chapter Six. They each experienced a powerful energy pulsing through them at a very rapid and high frequency.

Several hours later, I was driving home from lunch when my cell phone rang. It was Wayne Dyer asking permission to use my orb photo in his new book, *Wishes Fulfilled*, just three days from his book deadline. I was stunned as my mind instantly cataloged all of the synchronistic events that had to have happened in order for me to arrive at this exact moment in time.

My experience tells me that nothing happens by accident. With passion and intention, I focused my thoughts on moving the orb message forward. Wayne Dyer was on my mind daily, coupled with my strong intuition that he was somehow connected. Had I picked up, via the cosmic ether or Universal Mind, his focus on orbs?

Then, because we were both focused on the same subject, did the Universe bring us together? Was this all part of a greater plan, a pre-birth plan, which included the death of my son as a catalyst for my participation?

My orb photograph and a link to my website ended up in a book written by a well-known and respected self-help guru. It was his first book that included the subject of orbs. The book would introduce orbs to a whole new segment of the population outside the spiritual and paranormal community. I was a part of that introduction.

Proof of Heaven

In April of 2012, I was introduced to Dr. Alexander at a conference in Phoenix. I was busy taking orb photographs of the speakers and missed Dr. Alexander's presentation. In fact, I completely missed the orb connection. Five months later, at a second conference in Phoenix, I had the opportunity to hear his presentation.

Even after listening to the story of Betsy, I didn't make the connection to Betsy as an orb until after he shared the galleys of his new book, *Proof of Heaven*. I was stunned. His experience with his birth sister, someone whom he had never met, and her appearance as a brilliant orb in his near-death experience, validated my theory, work and research that orbs are connected to our loved ones. I moved forward with full confidence that I was indeed on the right track.

Spirit had been driving me relentlessly for a reason. I had endured the raised brows, rolled eyes and outright dismissal by many academicians and others in the spiritual and afterlife fields. Thank God, I had been willing to listen to Spirit and participate in the greater unfolding plan, despite how crazy and difficult it seemed at the time.

Thank God I'd listened to my intuition, my *knowing*, and the divine guidance I was given to forge ahead despite the frosty reception and large obstacles I'd encountered along the way.

What I find even more interesting from this experience is the truth behind the message imparted by so many different sages, philosophers, authors, and spiritual leaders throughout the centuries: that we are all connected. We are just beginning to understand the mystery of how that connection functions.

I reviewed the sequence of events and series of so-called coincidences, connecting the dots between my original thought and the outcome. Was the experience with Wayne Dyer an example of the law of attraction and that what I focus on I attract? Was it a vibrational level on which I was resonating? Was it a pre-birth plan where I, along with the souls of Eben Alexander and Wayne Dyer, had collectively agreed to help awaken others to the existence of orbs, their connection to our loved ones, and our life as eternal beings?

Was Patricia Alexander, who insisted I attend the November conference with her, placed in my path to ensure my connection with Wayne? Did the producer of both conferences also unwittingly play a role in this unfolding drama by including my photo in the FedEx to Wayne?

Do we create every moment of our lives through our thoughts and vibration, and does the Universe respond in kind? Or is there also a greater plan that we agree to before we're born, for which we become witnesses as it continues to unfold before us?

When I realized that my son's death propelled me in this direction, I also realized that sometimes in the midst of a tragedy we cannot see the bigger picture and the wonderful gifts that may come from that experience.

By consciously choosing to view life from my authentic self 'S' instead of ego self 's', I have created a strong connection to God and His miracles. I have used my thoughts to raise my vibration and experienced the miracle of Spirit and power of manifestation. I have recognized and utilized the power inherent in all of us and consciously changed my grief journey from one of sadness to one of love and joy.

It has been challenging but well worth the effort. The Universe continues to offer me learning and forgiveness opportunities. The following is one such experience. I had a choice. I chose love.

Choose Love

Several months ago, I received a very angry and accusatory email about my work with the orb phenomenon. The woman stated among other things that orbs were just dust and moisture and I was taking advantage of people through my orb website. My heart sank as I read the email. For a brief moment, the skeptical part of me reared its head and questioned the truth behind the orb phenomenon.

Were they real or was I just imagining all of this? Fear and doubt crept in, but I slammed the brakes on that negative thinking. I knew orbs were real from my experiences with them. I realized that the author of the email may have suffered a terrible loss of a loved one and was lashing out at me because she was unable to find a place of balance.

Although I felt compassion for her, I also realized that we all have free will. The only thing I could do was share the knowledge and experiences I've had that have helped in my healing. It was up to her to create her own grief journey and experience. I wrote a very kind and neutral email back and was met with even more viciousness. Instead of engaging with someone who was clearly angry and deliberately trying to pick a fight, I deleted the email, sent her love and light and moved forward.

While my friends jumped to my defense, it wasn't until the next morning that I was able to clearly see the gift delivered by her email. I'm grateful that her angry email gave me the opportunity to choose love. It would have been easy to become angry and defensive, but I now know in every experience, including the death of my son, there are lessons and gifts.

By choosing love instead of anger, I feel that I was rewarded that evening with one of the few sleep state ADCs or after-death communications I've had with orbs. I extend my gratitude to the angry stranger for facilitating the opportunity for my ADC by choosing love.

Since I started this journey, I have only had a handful of orb ADCs. I have also had a handful of ADCs with Chris. During this particular ADC, it was evening and I was standing with my oldest son on a patio. As I turned to my right to give him a hug and tell him how much I loved him, my heart swelled with unconditional love.

The overwhelming feeling of someone standing in the garden observing us pulled my attention back to my left. As I turned, I watched in awe as hundreds of orbs materialized above the manicured garden that was softly lit and filled with neatly trimmed boxwood hedges and fragrant gardenia bushes. Equally spaced but varying in size, the gossamer orbs, rimmed with thin black lines and a golden sheen in the center, floated effortlessly in space as if buoyed by an invisible wave.

Each orb contained a face, a testament to the unique individual it represented. I was overwhelmed and humbled by their appearance. "Oh my God, look at all the orbs. You're real. Can you see them too?" I whispered to my son.

He said, "Yes, Mom. I can see them too."

I watched as I grew and changed into someone I didn't recognize. Struggling to understand the meaning of this I began to look at the other orbs to see if I could recognize their faces. At that point, my ADC ended. After I awoke, I lay quietly for several minutes, reviewing each detail of my experience with the orbs. In that moment, I realized the ease with which we can lose sight of our authentic selves here in this dimension. Even at her core, the woman who sent the angry email is still love and divine light, buried beneath the hurts and disappointments she has experienced in this lifetime.

Photo 98 © Monika Moehwald-Doelz. Orbs in the garden.

Each of us struggles to find our authentic self so we can learn to respond from that place of childlike innocence and love. Children are a beautiful example of authentic selfhood. They are fresh from God, Source, I Am Presence; a reminder of the joy and unconditional love we all possess at birth that often becomes misdirected or misguided as we move through life's challenges.

CHAPTER TEN

"The fairies went from the world, dear, because men's
hearts grew cold: And only the eyes of children see
what is hidden from the old."

~ Kathleen Foyle

Children and Orbs

My first visual experience regarding the idea of an orb was in the movie, *The Wizard of Oz*. You may recall the scene where Glinda, the good witch of the North, arrives inside a beautiful ball of light. It appears in the distance about the size of a volley ball and as it approaches Dorothy, it grows large enough to contain an adult.

Inside the transparent ball of light is a woman who manifests into a life-sized guardian angel. When I first saw *The Wizard of Oz* at the age of six, I was too young to realize the significance of this scene. It represented a ball of light as a vessel for the embodiment of the human spirit and a combination of magic, wonder, consciousness, and protection. These are many of these attributes I found to be true during the last several years of my research and experiences with orbs.

During the 2013 National IANDS Conference in Crystal City, Virginia, I met Peter Shockey, the Producer/Director of the award-winning documentary, *Life After Life*. He brought to my attention that the *Wizard of Oz* is a wonderful example of a near-death experience.

Dorothy is knocked unconscious, travels through a tunnel portrayed by a tornado, and experiences the hyper-vivid world on the other side.

Much to my delight, I quickly made the leap that if this were true it meant that Glinda arrived in an orb! I realized this movie had been filmed years before I was born and decades before the invention of the digital camera. I wondered if the author had had a near-death experience at some point in their life.

My quest to discover the identity of these intriguing balls of light continues to be orchestrated by synchronistic events. Many times, a direct question to the orbs themselves was followed shortly by a suggestion from a friend or acquaintance to read a specific book.

Although the general contents of each book seemed to have nothing to do with orbs, hidden between the pages were pieces of a much larger puzzle. Eagerly I dove into each book, knowing that somewhere within a matter of hours, more information about the identity of these orbs would be revealed to me.

One summer day, I was enjoying a luncheon on the patio of my Aunt Susan's house with children's author, Delores Desio, when I mentioned my son Chris and my orb research. She knit her brows for a moment and then said that she happened to have in her car a children's book about angels. For some reason she thought I needed to read it. Later that evening I settled into bed and came upon a story about an orb.

Marigo

New York Times bestselling author Joan Wester Anderson writes about people and their encounters with angels. In her book, *An Angel to Watch Over Me: True Stories of Children's Encounters with Angels,* Joan tells the story of a little boy who sees a ball of light come in through his closed window and turn into a lady.[75] His mother encourages him to ask the lady's name if she returns, and to find out more about her.

The following night the ball of light returns to the little boy's room. The lady tells him that she loves him and that she is his angel. Her name is Marigo. He draws a picture of her for his parents, but she is without wings or a halo. Over a period of years, Marigo visits him many times, arriving through a "closed window in a large round circle of light."

Many of us have heard stories of youngsters talking with their deceased grandmother or grandfather, or even with their imaginary friends. Although it sounds wonderful in theory, how do we really know for sure that what they see or experience isn't a large part of their imagination? Could these experiences be real?

Sarah

Peter Shockey, author of *Reflections of Heaven: A Millennial Odyssey of Miracles, Angels, and Afterlife,* shares the story of fourteen-year-old Sarah Powell who is the victim of a teenage gang that breaks into her home.[76] Hit on the head by her assailant, she leaves her body and arrives in a heavenly paradise, met by a school chum who died four days earlier. He tells her she must return, but first she must meet her guardian angel, George, who is dressed in a white suit and top hat and speaks with a British accent.

George says she will be fine and it isn't time yet to die. She feels comforted by him. When she returns to her body, the assault leaves her with total amnesia. Her recovery is slow and a month after the crime she begins to suffer grand mal seizures. During the seizures, the terrifying memories of the crime return. Sarah works with a therapist named Sharon to help her deal with her painful memories. Directly after a seizure, Sharon happens to call. Sarah says:

> While I was talking to Sharon, a light appeared before me. At first, it was a circular shape and then it came down to be a long oval. And it was…well, I knew that it was the one I had met under the tree when I died! It was George. I

immediately stopped crying, and Sharon, the psychologist, just seemed amazed.

She asked, "Why did you calm down so quickly?"

I answered, "Well, George says I'm going to be okay. He's going to take care of me now."

George instructs Sarah to tell her parents that "…when I was a little kid I used to laugh at him because he had this big hat that he always pushed away from his eyes."

Sarah's mother burst into tears as she remembers her daughter as a two and three-year-old. "Sarah would break into little bursts of laughter for no apparent reason. We'd peek into her room and say, 'What are you laughing at?' In a giggly voice, you would reply, "The man with the big hat comes and makes me laugh.'"[77]

Sarah's mother had saved the pictures that Sarah had drawn of the man she'd seen in the white tux and top hat. It was George, her guardian angel, and the same visitor Sarah remembered as a child.

Is it possible that we have been altogether too eager to disregard the notion that our children are able to see Spirit in action? Children are born with a strong connection to God, Source and I AM Presence and without the negative influences of this earthly third dimensional realm. It is possible that when their experiences are dismissed as imagination or they are exposed to an environment of fear, disbelief, dogma and criticism they lose this ability to communicate.

Imagine how different our world would be if we nurtured the gift of contact which our children were born with. For innocent inquisitive children, gentle questions and answers without criticism would make a wonderful environment in which to develop these gifts. Imagine the implications of possibly having our most sought after spiritual questions answered because we fostered these gifts.

Photo 99 (left) © Kati Scocchia. Little girl with an orb.
Photo 100 (right) © Mya Gleny. Infant staring at a squiggle.

Bye-Bye

Most people dismiss the notion that children are born with the ability to communicate with the other side. In fact, many children can see or feel orbs nearby. The little girl in Photo 99 is almost two years old. Her mother, Kati, took this picture in February 2013 while on vacation. It shows the child looking at the orb above her arm. Katie says:

> We were at a restaurant and both kids kept running back and forth down a long stretch of the restaurant, just being happy. I find much more orb activity in the pictures when there is joy and happiness. The kids were just being happy, loving the warm night air, and interacting with people when I captured this photo of my daughter staring at an orb.
>
> She's not quite old enough for me to ask her questions about them but I do hear her say "bye-bye" to what appears to me to be just air. Once, she pointed to an orb picture and said, "Baby." She has also stared at the ceiling as if she's watching something."

Charlie

Mya Gleny is a writer, painter, photographer and author of *Orbs: The Gift of Light.*[78] She shared this photo taken with her grandson, Charlie. Photo 100 shows the baby is staring directly at the moving squiggle.

He appears to be contemplating whether or not he could reach out and touch it. This squiggle seems oddly similar to the description Erica McKenzie mentioned earlier.

With Erica's ability to see both orbs and "squiggles," we now know that the "squiggle" is altogether different from an "orb," although we can capture an orb in motion, which can look similar to a "squiggle." Mya's story that follows is a testament to the validity of the orb phenomenon and our children's ability to connect with the beauty and wonder of Spirit. Mya says:

> Charlie is now one and a half, and in July 2012, he and I were sitting on the floor in my house playing. Charlie was eating some grapes. Suddenly, he looked up at the empty doorway as if someone had just appeared. He offered up a grape to the unseen someone. I said, "Is it an angel, Charlie?" He popped the grape into his mouth and looked at me with his huge baby eyes.
>
> "Why don't you give the angel a grape, Charlie?" I said.
>
> He offered up another grape, and then snatched it back and giggled as if someone was playing a game with him. He offered it up again and did the same thing, giggling again. Then he watched something move across the room to the window. He turned to me and said, "Bubble."

Owen

On August 20, 2012, Jenn Kephart was lying on a beanbag and talking with her fiancé, who sat in a recliner to her right. They had just finished watching a movie. Jenn says:

> My son Owen, who was sixteen-months old at the time, walked toward me from the left. Just as I turned to look at Owen, I saw a white orb float horizontally from right to left in a downward angle from the ceiling. It was a solid white ball—very white but not bright. It didn't glow nor did it

flicker. It was the size of a small, bouncy ball that comes from a twenty-five cent machine.

The orb came from the right about six feet away and was about eight feet from the ground. It was visible for only a second. It descended quickly and disappeared behind his head as he stepped in front of me. Instinctively, I followed the trajectory toward the couch where it would have continued onward had it appeared from behind Owen's head.

Owen stood directly in front of me as I sat up in the beanbag. My fiancé, son and I chatted for a few minutes until Owen looked to my left. He acted as if he was seeing something or someone on the couch, which would have been where the orb would have come to rest.

He responded the way a child would if a stranger were coaxing him to come over to them. He made a face and stared at the couch for about twenty seconds. I was so taken by his interaction that I even looked in the direction of the couch to see what was causing Owen such concern.

My fiancé doesn't believe in the paranormal so I didn't mention anything to him, but he was aware that Owen's reaction was a little weird. Owen then became scared and crawled up into my lap for comfort. He did not cry. He continued to look in the direction of the couch as we lay stomach to stomach for a few seconds. He then turned his head away, gave me a kiss and continued onto something else. On New Year's Eve 2012, I heard Owen call out "bubble."

Brooklyn's "Bubbles"

In February of 2014, I placed my nineteen-month-old granddaughter, Brooklyn, on the changing table and chatted with her as I changed her diaper. She babbled back at me and then suddenly something above her caught her attention. She pointed at it, followed it with her head and eyes and said, "Ball."

Instantly, I knew she had seen an orb. There's a certain thrill I get watching my granddaughter discover orbs. It was as if all the stories and photos I had collected suddenly had new meaning. Here was a toddler whom we had never introduced to orbs, and suddenly she was following something that was invisible to me yet obviously visible to her, and describing it by saying "ball."

At twenty-three months old, Brooklyn's vocabulary and experiences had increased. One day, she was scooting down the staircase on her tummy, feet first. Kristin was standing at the top of the stairs holding four-month-old Ryland. Brooklyn pointed off to the side of her mother's head and said, "Bubble!" Once Kristin had descended the stairs, passing Brooklyn, the toddler pointed toward her again and said, "More bubble." Kristin knew immediately that Brooklyn had seen orbs.

A bubble is a great description for an orb. Orbs can look like delicate gossamer bubbles floating through the air when filmed on an infrared video camera. I find it interesting that very young children would come up with the same word "bubble" to describe an invisible presence.

Amelia

During lunch at a seminar in Las Vegas in January 2012, I met Sarah. As I proceeded to talk about orbs with my friends, Sarah, who happened to be sharing the couch with us in a small coffee shop, asked me if the orbs scared me.

"Not in the least," I assured her. "I've only experienced wonderful interactions with them."

It wasn't until Sarah returned home later that weekend that our discussion jogged her memory of an interesting incident with her youngest daughter when she was around five or six years of age. Sarah recalls her daughter mentioning dots:

My daughter told me one day that she couldn't sleep the night before because of the dots. I stared at her very confused and asked, "What dots?"

She said, "You know the dots, the dots, the dots!" She pointed everywhere.

My husband and I looked at each other like she was crazy and let it go. She was angry when we couldn't see them. We always thought it was a funny story to tell friends. Amelia and her imagination!

She is eighteen now and tells me that she still sees tons of these "dots" all around her most of the time. None of them are colored and they are all very small. She knows that no one else can see them so she doesn't talk about them.

Jack and Ben

During Christmas 2010, I was visiting my family. My brother and sister-in-law had come for dinner and afterward, my twelve-year-old nephew, Jack, begged me to take orb pictures with him. He bounced back and forth on tiptoes like he had to run to the bathroom and exclaimed, "I know where they are, Aunt Shelly. Come on!" Shelly is my nickname.

"Really, Jack? You know where they are?" I asked with a raised brow.

"Yes. They are back in the guest bedroom where you're staying. Hurry up and let's go get them!" He pulled me in the direction of the bedroom.

"I wanna come too, Aunt Shelly," pleaded Benjamin.

Benjamin is Jack's eight-year-old brother. I said okay and grabbed my camera. We hurried off toward the guest bedroom.

The guest room is large enough for two queen beds. All three of us huddled together on the one farthest from the door. We turned off the lights and I started to take pictures while we watched the small camera screen for any signs of orb activity. We immediately saw them zipping through the infrared of our camera just before the flash fired. The boys squealed with delight.

Our first shot consisted of multiple-colored and white moving orbs. I snapped a few more pictures and then Benjamin asked if he could try. We continued to get some very active orb pictures. We paused for a moment and then turned on the lights to review our pictures.

Jack jumped up off the bed and asked, "Do you think they like music?" He reached for the radio on the side of the nightstand and turned it on. "Maybe they like to dance!"

"Maybe," I answered.

"I'm going to stand by the door and you take pictures of me," said Jack.

"Me too!" Benjamin leaped off the bed and followed his brother.

"Put up your hands and maybe you can catch one," I called out then turned off the lights and began to take pictures.

The boys cried out in unison, "I can see them!"

I could also see them as they lit up with the flash of the camera. Suddenly, Benjamin ran over and dove onto the bed next to me, belly first, and hid his face in his hands. I stopped taking pictures and patted his back. "Benjamin, are you okay?" He didn't answer.

"Ben, what's the matter?" I asked again, and then turned on the light while he continued to hide his face. "Ben, what is it?"

"I felt one on my head. It was in my hair," he answered from the depths of the pillow.

"It was in your hair? Wow! You felt it?"

I reviewed the last picture. There it was. An orb the size of a soft ball was sitting on Benjamin's head.

He sat up and looked at the photo, suddenly quite proud of the shot. Then he rolled over onto his back, closed his eyes and lay very still. Jack chimed in and asked me to take more pictures of him, since he could see them zooming around the darkened room when the camera flashed.

I looked down at Benjamin and wondered what he was doing.

He whispered, "I can feel them, Aunt Shelly. They're touching me."

"That's so cool, Ben. I want to feel them touching me, too," I said. He stayed next to me while I turned out the lights and began taking photos of Jack.

Suddenly, out of the dark Jack yelled, "I almost caught one! Check the camera!" (Photo 101)

Photo 101 (left) © Trying to catch an orb. Photo 102 (right) Benjamin manifesting an orb above his head. © Virginia Hummel.

We turned on the lights again as I reviewed the last few pictures. There it was, directly above Jack's raised hands. The expression on my nephew's face was one of pure joy. In the original photo, there are nearly twenty orbs in varying stages of fluorescence.

That Christmas, I gifted Ben and Jack with "orb" cameras, since they showed such an interest in the subject. Jack could even tell me where to shoot with the lights on, just by sensing their presence.

During Thanksgiving 2012, my nephew, Ben wanted me to take orb photos as he attempted to manifest an orb above his head. My brother and niece jumped in the photo too, but I got the feeling my brother was making fun of me. Interestingly enough, in Photo 102 he is looking right at the orb above Ben's head. There are several other orbs in the photo.

Photo 103 © Virginia Hummel. Kristin identifies the orb above her head as her unborn child.

Kristin's "Little Bubble"

My older daughter Kristin was visited by Spirit at a very young age and I seized the opportunity to foster these abilities in my family. Her connection to Spirit was very strong and I tried to be especially encouraging in the way I would answer her questions. Over the course of the last four or five years,

Kristin would tell me about a little orb that she would see hanging around her. She identified it as the soul of a child she would eventually have. Several holistic body workers would comment when they performed work on my daughter that two children were hovering nearby, waiting to be born.

She acknowledged the presence of both of them. In May of 2012, we were out to dinner with family. My daughter was seven months pregnant with Brooklyn when I took Photo 103.

A beautiful little orb appears above her head in the photo. Instantly she said, "See, Mom, that's the little orb I was telling you about. She's waiting to be born and pops in and out of my belly!"

Carmel

Euphrates S. contacted me in March of 2013 with this email about her young daughter, Carmel:

> I recently came across your website and became absolutely fascinated with your story and the images you took of the orbs. What led me to find your website was the search for answers. You see, a year ago my five-year-old daughter told me she can see "balls of energy." We were in her room one night getting ready for bedtime and she suddenly looked up and said, "Mommy, do you see them too?" I looked up and couldn't see anything. I asked her what did she see, and she continued to explain that she sees ball of energy in different colors.
>
> Other parents may have brushed it off as their child's imagination, but having been very intuitive myself, I knew my little girl spoke the truth. I told her they were the star people Spirits and that they were there to protect her. She found comfort in that and felt safe as she lay down to sleep.
>
> She is now a year older. She is learning different shapes in school. A few days ago, she told me that the orbs she sees come in different shapes. They are not only circular but also triangular, square and rectangular prisms. She sees them mostly in pink and red.
>
> I decided to do some more research and that is when I came across your website. When I showed her the images on your website, she said that is exactly what she sees. She was so excited that there was proof that what she sees is absolutely real and not all in her mind.
>
> That night we also experimented with our own camera and actually captured some orbs. They were very small but I was amazed that even though I always felt it, I was finally able to see what it was my daughter was seeing.

She says she feels happiness when she sees them. And yes, she sees the squiggle snake like ones as well. She also says she sees funny looking eight shaped orbs. I'm assuming they look like the infinity sign. I asked her if she sees the same ones.

She said she thinks they are the same ones but she's not sure because they change their shapes and colors. Yesterday, she said she saw a blue one with a ring of rainbow colors around it. My camera doesn't capture that at all. The ones I can see are very small and white. Like small and round jellyfish.

In June 2013, Euphrates sent me an email: She wrote, "I wanted to update you on our experiences since we last spoke. My daughter, having been very aware of the orbs now, is telling me she is starting to see their faces."

Little Voices

It is important to address the effects that spiritual phenomena can have on children. I am not a licensed psychologist, counselor or therapist. As parents we must all do what we feel is in the best interest of our children, and as such, please seek help from a health care professional if necessary.

The following information is my opinion and is one of many ways to consider handling issues that arise from children and their experiences from spiritual encounters.

Children look to their parents for guidance and safety. As parents, we try our best to protect our children from danger. We wouldn't hesitate to grab our child to keep them from running into the street, just as we would proactively listen to and believe our child if they told us a stranger had approached them in an inappropriate way. But what if our child is telling us about something that frightens them that we can't see?

In the past, our initial response to children may have been to laugh it off, explain it away, ignore it, or outright deny what they are telling

130

us. Sometimes we just don't know what to do. Unfortunately, as humans we generally tend to revert to fear or denial when presented with a situation that we don't understand.

Recently, I received an email from a mother whose four-year-old daughter claims there is a man in her room. Each night at two o'clock AM she awakens terrified and she crawls into her mother's bed. During a visit from a psychic, she has pointed to the man standing in her room.

As parents and adults how could we best help this child?

First, I suggest that we honor and validate her feelings as well as her experience by listening carefully to what she is telling us, and then take her seriously. If we are afraid or do not understand what is happening, then we should seek out someone who can help us. *Under no circumstances should we disregard, make fun of or ignore a child's plea for help.* These are real experiences and we can be proactive in helping our children to understand and deal with them in a positive way.

We can begin by calmly asking her questions. Knowledge is power. The more you know about the stranger, the better you will be able to deal with them. Get a description of the individual. What do they look like? How old are they? (Relatives may appear much younger than during their last moments when we knew them.) What are they wearing? Do they talk? What do they say? How do they frighten you? Have they hurt you? Do they only come at night? Do you see anything or anyone else? And so on. If the child is too young to speak, modify your questions so they can answer by nodding, shaking their head "no" or pointing to something similar.

Above all, we should be supportive, comforting and protective of our child and make sure they know of our willingness to help them through a disquieting situation.

One of the first things that I suggest is to pull out the family photo album. Without leading your child, let them look carefully at the photos to see if they recognize the person who is visiting them. Sometimes an earlier photo of the person is necessary for recognition.

You may have to borrow albums from older relatives who have family photos from previous generations when they were younger looking.

A friend of mine had a toddler who was talking with someone in her room. I suggested using a photo album to identify the visitor. Before she had a chance to consider my suggestion, the toddler pointed to a family photo hanging in the hallway. The toddler, who was too young to speak, identified my friend's mother, who had passed away many years before, as the woman in her room.

My friend was comforted, knowing her mother was there with her daughter, and then proceed to tell her stories about her grandmother. If the photo albums aren't working, then you may want to investigate the history of the house and those who lived there before.

Many people are sensitive to the energy left behind when a person crosses over. There is a difference between a ghost and a person who has crossed over who appears as an orb. Julia Assante, Ph.D., is a professional intuitive, medium and author of *The Last Frontier: Exploring the Afterlife and Transforming Our Fear of Death*.[79] Julia states:

> Ghosts are associated with a specific place. They are also characterized by repetitious movements, much like the reruns of a video clip....A ghost is only a portion of the core self...What makes a ghost imprint is usually a combination of a person's extreme emotion and obsessive-compulsive thought.[80]

On occasion, other individuals or entities that may not be welcome in your home can also appear. We have the ability to demand that they leave and then set up a psychic or spiritual wall of protection around our loved ones.

Whether you are spiritual or religious, you can call in divine love and light to surround your loved ones while visualizing a protective shield of white or violet light around them. You can intentionally create a barrier between yourselves and these entities.

When I was eight or nine-years-old, my parents moved me from my younger brother's room to my own. I remember being terrified to sleep alone in my room at night. I would build a fort with dozens of stuffed animals around me to hide from "them." I cannot recall exactly who "they" were, but the feeling of visitation was and is still quite real. In fact, I slept with a light on until I was thirty-five-years old.

As a child, my father would come to tuck me in bed and tell me a story to help allay my fears. The story was about a young girl with a magic handkerchief that could protect her from harm. While I clung tightly each night to the handkerchief he gave me, I continued to encounter that same distinct feeling that "they" would come to visit.

As I grew, I became aware of my gifts and sensitivities to Spirit. I realized that what I had experienced as a child was real. I also realized how comforting it would have been had I encountered knowledgeable parents who were able to help me understand what was happening and how to deal with it.

If you are having difficulty, you can contact a reputable psychic or medium and have them assist you. I always ask those family members on the other side for their help and assistance with this. I also call heavily on God, Jesus, my guides and angels. Remember, when the little voice of your child calls out, please listen and respond in a compassionate, proactive way.

Remember…
It is possible for children to sense orbs and Spirit.
It is possible for children to feel orbs and Spirit.
It is possible for children to see orbs and Spirit.
So, nurture and encourage your child's abilities.

CHAPTER ELEVEN

"The moment you doubt whether you can fly,
You cease forever to be able to do it."

~ J.M. Barrie, Peter Pan

Orbs and Adults

Rarely do we question a child who describes angels, orbs and fairies, because we expect children to have active imaginations. However, when adults begin to describe experiences that include the supernormal, many of us grab our skeptic hats and often have a difficult time controlling wry comments or snickers that translate to "What kind of Kool-Aid is she drinking?"

We are much too uncomfortable discussing things we can't see or haven't yet experienced ourselves. I have been guilty of this because frankly, I am a still a skeptic at heart.

Does the fact that we are uncomfortable with the conversation make a spiritual experience any less real? We are learning that some people have the ability to see these brilliant balls of light or "orbs" without the aid of a camera.

The following accounts are from people of all walks of life. Some came to me through a friend or an acquaintance and others found their way into this book via the website that Spirit insisted I create.

Photo 104 © Monica Gilbert Flores in a cloud of orbs.

Drunvalo

Drunvalo Melchizedek is the author of four books, which include *The Ancient Secret of the Flower of Life, Volumes I & II, Living in the Heart*, and *Serpent of Light*.[81] These books have been published in twenty-nine languages, with readers in more than one hundred countries.

He is a consultant for the international Internet magazine, *Spirit of Ma'at*, with over one million viewers each year, and the founder of the Flower of Life Facilitators who have been teaching his work in over sixty countries around the world.

In his book, *The Serpent of Light: Beyond 2012 The Movement of the Earth's Kundalini and the Rise of the Female Light, 1949-2013*, he states: "In 1971, two softly glowing spheres of light, one bright green and the other an ultraviolet color, entered into the room where I was meditating and identified themselves by saying, 'We are not separate from you. We are you.'"[82]

Carol

Carol Adler is President and CEO of Dandelion Books. We met in 2011 when I needed an editor for my first book. I loved the way she was able to use her spiritual background in the editing process. I received an email from her one day as she began editing process for this book and came across Amelia's story in the children's section. It jogged a memory of childhood and a similar experience long forgotten. Carol says:

> When I was very small, I would lie awake at night watching all the colored dots that danced before my eyes, everywhere. They appeared every night. When I told my parents about them, they were worried about my eyesight and took me to an eye doctor.

> My eyes were perfectly fine. They said I was just imagining them and eventually they went away. When I was forty-nine, I experienced a major crisis that led to a healing. One of my psychic counselors who became a "sister" to me, said, "Those dots were very real. They are living beings. You are always surrounded by them."

> It's amazing that we really don't have to "see" the orbs to know they're there with us, all the time. Everywhere. Infinite numbers of them.

Diandra

In October of 2012, I gave a presentation on orbs at the Foundation for Mind-Being Research in Palo Alto, California.[83] During the question and answer period afterward, Diandra Wood shared a story with the audience that occurred some thirty to thirty-five years ago. Diandra says:

> I was in my early twenties and one night my husband and I were lying in bed talking in the dark. There was no external source of light and the drapes were closed, along with the bedroom door. All of a sudden, over his nightstand, this brilliant ball of light showed up. It just blinked in.

> It didn't appear to come from anywhere and it stayed for twenty minutes. We timed it. We got up and looked at it. It was very dense and opaque, but very bright white and we

couldn't see through it. It was approximately five inches in diameter and glowed light out from it a little bit.

We put our hands up to it and discovered there was no heat or cold emanating from it. We didn't feel anything nor did we hear anything. It didn't move but remained in a solid, steady state.

We wondered if it was somehow trying to communicate with us. We weren't feeling any malevolence from the orb and both agreed with the impression that it was observing us. Then just as suddenly as it appeared, it blinked out.

Amanda

Amanda Stone was staying with a friend after a Reiki[84] session and slept on her sofa that night with her Chihuahua. She says:

I woke up and walked to the window to watch the rain and check out a storm. I lay back down and I must not have been asleep long (maybe fifteen minutes) when I heard a loud whirring noise that woke me up.

As I opened my eyes, I saw a ball of light inches from my face. It was smaller than my head with what looked like spinning twine encircling the light and spinning in every direction. The noise that woke me up was the sound of the twine moving and spinning around the light.

I looked at Winston. The Chihuahua was staring at it too as it was in the middle of the two of us. I felt very relaxed and matter of fact about it. I don't know how long I stared at it but then it disappeared.

My reaction was a little strange as well. I wasn't even that much in awe. It was more like, "Huh, look at that." Anyway, it appeared three-dimensional and my friend thinks it was an ET. I have no idea what it was, but I do feel as though I was being checked out by something.

Marcie

Marcie York had been going through a devastating personal experience and had been praying for a personal visitation from Jesus. On this particular night after praying, she asked for Jesus to send angels if He was not going to visit her. She writes:

> My husband was asleep when I crawled into bed. Just as I was starting to drift off to sleep, I was awakened by bright white balls of light. They were coming through my bedroom ceiling following a straight white beam of light entering my head, moving down into my chest and then out through my head and back up the beam of light and exiting through my ceiling. There were hundreds of them by the time the night was done; they moved as if they were on an invisible conveyor belt.

> I could feel the white light building in me so much that you could see it starting to radiate out of my body. I was filled with such happiness and joy like I have never experienced in my entire life. There really are no words to truly describe it accurately. It was non-stop for six hours. I watched the clock and turned from side to side as needed for comfort.

> I wanted my husband to wake up and see what was going on but he continued to sleep throughout the night, which is so out of character for him. I wanted to wake him but somehow knew that if I did, the balls of white light would stop and it was so glorious, I didn't want them to. Finally, after six hours, I could no longer contain my excitement and I jumped up onto my knees and shook him awake, everything stopped when I did this.

> I felt as if they were angels entering into my broken heart and depositing good while taking out the bad when leaving; a sort of healing. I've never seen anything in the Bible talking about white balls of light, but everything in my head and heart say that it was of God, whatever it was.

Photo 105 was discovered on Facebook and reminded me of the streaming orbs in Marci's story.

Photo 105 © Juan Carlos Ramirez Ibarra. A man standing in a stream of orbs.

Brent

In a telephone interview, Brent C. of Cupertino, California told me of an experience he had one evening in an office building off Scott Boulevard in Santa Clara, California. Brent says:

> I was accompanied by two friends who had heard over the years that the building was haunted. Workers on the building claimed to have seen and heard strange things. My friends and I decided to do a "sit-in" between the hours of 9 p.m. and midnight one evening to see if the rumors we'd heard were true.

> We took our places in different parts of the building and waited. Some office lights were on and others were off. I sat in the corridor and suddenly noticed an orb the size of a ping-pong ball floating down the hallway. It would briefly disappear when it reached the lighted sections of the hallway.

It floated approximately one foot off the ground, bouncing in mid-air, rising and falling as it approached me. It was fuzzy white, like a cotton ball. Two of the three of us who were there that night witnessed this orb. I also heard voices, like two people having a muffled conversation down the hallway, just out of earshot. I knew it wasn't my friends.

I saw the orb for one to three-minute intervals during a fifteen-minute period. I also felt the presence of someone. I didn't feel any fear, just curiosity and interest as to what it might be.

Pat

A woman named Pat emailed me describing an encounter she had with a little orb during a medical procedure and how it affected her. Pat writes:

> The first time I saw an orb was during a medical procedure two and a half years ago. I was a gestational carrier for a girlfriend and her husband, and right before the transfer of their embryo into my womb, I saw an orb about the size of a large coin up above to my right. I felt no fear.
>
> I just watched it for a moment and felt comforted and an unspoken understanding. After thinking about it, I felt that it was either the baby's spirit, preparing to enter the physical form inside me, or my Grandmother who has passed on there to support me at the time.

Ivy

Ivy Wigmore sent me an email describing several different types of orbs she has seen in various colors and circumstances during the day and evening. She writes:

> My first experience seeing an orb was watching my neighbor out walking his dog. He's a lovely, laid-back man who seems

to be fully immersed in the present, in a good space. He just rambles along in no hurry, no worry.

Anyway, as I drove past him one day he was strolling along taking in the world and a golden orb floated along with him. I got a very maternal feeling from it. It was about the size of a basketball. I learned from his wife later that he had been very close to his mother who has been dead for some years.

The second time I saw an orb was when my husband and I were in bed. We'd just returned from his mom's interment and I saw a blue orb beside him, I would guess about the size of a baseball.

In both cases, I had the sense that there were details to be seen but I didn't see the orbs for long enough to catch any, probably just a few seconds in the first case and a couple in the second. I thought this was probably his mum but I think was mostly just because we'd buried her ashes that day rather than any strong feeling I got about the orb itself.

Another time, I was running downstairs from my office to answer the door, and as I was running, I could see what seemed to be an orb of white light over my head. It kept pace with me, almost like it was a balloon attached to me. I also see tiny silvery orbs quite often, just in front of me.

One time as I was waking up I saw a small and more intensely blue orb come into the bedroom very quickly and hover briefly in front of my husband and then briefly in front of me.

I also saw a small deep orange orb zipping around my house, watched it duck behind a speaker, and zip into the bathroom. One time, I watched it entered my abdomen, it's probably not something it should have been able to do.

I've seen a number of other deeper blue orbs that seem different somehow. I've seen these ones swoop up to windows of houses as I passed them and once perched in the top of a tree outside my window shortly after the death of a very dear former lover.

After reading these stories and others I've encountered during my research, I have come to the conclusion that orb sightings are much more common than we suspect. I have hundreds of additional stories in my Inbox. Some people would initially approach me with a general email to test my response to an experience with orbs. Once I reassured them, the floodgates opened and I was privileged to read some incredible experiences.

I have always felt compelled to share my experiences with Spirit, regardless of the reaction they generate. I seem to find a way to strike up a conversation with the person next to me and inevitably, after a moment of silence, they share a wonderful experience they've kept secret for fear of being labeled crazy.

A feeling of relief washes over them as I patiently listen and reassure them they are anything but crazy. It is all so amazing and miraculous, yet I still find myself questioning my own sanity on occasion when encountering yet another unexpected spiritual event.

Dude! You're in My Face

In December 2010, I woke from a terrifying dream to find an orb the size of a volleyball sitting on my chest. "Dude! You're in my face!" flew out of my mouth. These words had no effect on my orb friend who was resting on the covers, six inches from my chin.

Never having uttered these words to a living soul before, I frankly don't know what possessed me to say them, other than the fact that the orb was so close. I was instantly jolted to a state of clarity and alertness and pulled my chin into my chest to create a few more inches of space between the two of us.

Staring at the orb, my terrifying dream was momentarily forgotten. Was I actually seeing it? To make certain, several times I glanced from the orb into the darkness of the room lit by the ambient light from my alarm key pad. Yes, there was an orb sitting on my chest. I forced myself to remain calm as I stared in awe, studying it carefully.

There was no fear, only curiosity and restrained excitement at this Being resting on my chest. I noted that it did not rise with my breath, nor did my chest or the bed sheet enter into the orb. It appeared to be present in my dimension, yet not of this dimension. Keeping my physical body perfectly still, I proceeded to study it. With a scientist's eye, I rigorously examined, recorded, and cataloged in detail every aspect of the orb.

Memorizing its shape, size and colors, I compared it to phenomena that existed in my third dimensional world. I observed it had a dark ring, like a black band, around its perimeter, that was approximately a quarter inch thick. Inside the band was a receptacle that resembled a living, three-dimensional fish tank. Swimming inside this "tank" were tiny entities that looked like worms, approximately the size and thickness of my thumb—about two-and-a-half inches in length and one inch in diameter.

At once, I was filled with questions. Was there really an orb on my chest? Where did it come from? Why was it here? Was it good or bad? Could it read my mind? Was I afraid of it? Would it harm me? Could I touch it? Would it let me? What was it made of? What would it feel like? Would I scare it away? Was it my son, and if not, who or what was it? Was it an extraterrestrial? Did it awaken me from my bad dream? Did it give me that dream?

Think, think.

It was the opportunity of a lifetime. What could I learn from the orb that I could share with my peers? What could it teach me? Is it always near me, even though I can't see it? Does it watch me while I sleep? Is it here every night?

Finally, the questions stopped pouring in and I continued to simply observe the orb. To my amazement, I felt as if it was also watching and observing me. In a moment of self-reflection, I was aware that I was emotionally neutral about the orb. It appeared neither masculine nor feminine, however, intuitively I thought of it as masculine.

What secrets might I discover that I could share with those who shared my passion and curiosity about orbs? Focusing on the right side of the orb, I watched the wormlike entities swim around inside the "fish tank." Even though the room was dark, I could still make out their bright neon "Play-Doh" like colors.

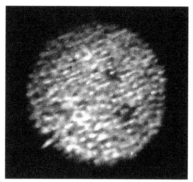

Photo 106 © Naomi Fugiwara. An orb
similar to what I saw resting on my chest.

With a slow, deliberate motion I slid my right arm from beneath the covers, lifted it above the orb and then, as if I were karate chopping it, carefully ran my hand through the orb, twice. This investigation didn't seem to deter the orb in the least. If the orb had been a balloon, the pressure of my hand would have altered its shape. Not so with the orb. Both its shape and the contents inside remained completely undisturbed.

In fact, my hand passed completely through it without affecting it in the least. I felt no sensation, no heat or cold, nothing tingly…nothing. Nor was there any evidence of moisture that would usually appear after touching something that swims. I felt no shift in energy or even the slightest vibration. Clearly, the orb was patiently allowing me to satisfy my curiosity without interfering.

Had the orb had been responsible for my terrifying dream or did it rescue me from the dream by waking me up? The latter seemed more probable because I felt no fear in its presence. Easing my arm beneath the covers once again, I continued to watch it as I added more questions to my list. Slowly, a deep feeling of peace settled over me and soon I was fast asleep.

Later when I reflected on this visitation, I found it hard to believe that I actually fell into a deep sleep with a volleyball-sized orb fish tank sitting on my chest. How embarrassing, disappointing and uncharacteristic for a person like me, who was passionate to know everything about orbs! Often I would wake up in the middle of the night, unable to sleep as my mind reviewed the latest information I'd uncovered in my relentless search for answers to this great mystery.

As I continued to mull over the strangeness of this visitation, I concluded that the "fish tank orb" had deliberately put me back to sleep. Why?

The following morning, I described the orb and my experience to my friends and family, receiving the usual nods and "that's nice." This response no longer deterred me. A month later, I discovered and purchased a new book on orbs. The first page of the photo insert in *Orbs: Their Missions and Messages of Hope,*[85] by Klaus and Gundi Heinemann had an enlargement of an orb taken in a cathedral that looked *exactly* like my description of the orb fish tank. It was another validation that I was on the right track, and that my experience was not just an active imagination.

Yet, this orb was different from the brilliant ball of light I saw three years earlier. Imagine if we were able to set fear and judgment aside, find a place of balance, and with openness and acceptance, share our spiritual experiences. Not only might we gather enough information to answer our questions regarding the orb phenomenon and other spiritual events, we might just discover that the "supernormal" is actually normal.

Orb Photos 107, 108, 109 and 110 were taken by Juan Carlos Ramirez Ibarra. He has captured these orb photographs in preparation for the awakening of consciousness 2012 at a place called Hunab Ku on the old road to San Ignacio in the city of Aguascalientes, Mexico.

Juan has put together some wonderful YouTube videos of his orb photographs from the Hunab Ku location.[86] Photos with people and orbs are more common than not but are humans the only ones who have experiences with orbs?

Photo 107 (left), 108 (right) © Juan Carlos Ramirez Ibarra.

Photo 109 (left) Photo 110 (right) © Juan Carlos Ramirez Ibarra.

CHAPTER TWELVE

"God spelled backward is dog.
I pray I may be as loving and forgiving as both of them."
~ Virginia Hummel

Pets and Orbs

Many people are capturing orb photos with their pets. The animals have a wonderful way of alerting us to their presence, although not all pets respond to their arrival. Dogs may bark or become excited at the arrival of orbs and chase them through the house while cats may just follow them with their eyes or stare in the direction of the orb.

My dog Winnie became quite excited upon their arrival but my other two dogs, Petie and Gracie, were unfazed. Photo 111 shows Star the dog looking at an orb. His owner Nancy Myers says he likes to bat at them with his paws. Photo 112 is a cat staring at an orb.

Many people are devastated when their pet crosses over and have ask if pets can also appear as orbs. Photo 113 was taken at a friend's house six weeks after her beloved cat crossed over. She had requested that I take orb photos so that she might know that her cat was still with her. She burst into tears when she saw the picture on my camera. She said, "That is the exact place my cat used to curl up on my bed, right on top of my mail."

Photo 111 (left) © Nancy Myers. "Star" plays with an orb. Photo 112 (upper right). Cat & orb © Rick R. Photo 113 (lower right) © Virginia Hummel. An orb appears in the exact spot where a friend's deceased cat used to lay.

Photo 114 shows Miss Mollie barking at the arrival to two small orbs. This was the first time we noticed that she was sensitive to the arrival of orbs. Photo 115 shows Winnie the pug who was the first to alert me upon an orb's arrival each night. This dog was constantly alerting me to the presence of orbs. Gracie is lying next to her completely unfazed by its arrival.

Photo 116 is my dog Petie with an orb sitting on the chair next to him. In Photo 117 Winnie has an orb on her head with another one close by. Photo 118 was captured by a field camera, courtesy of Larry White Buffalo, and shows an owl with an orb. Photo 119 is of a St. Bernard with an orb above his head that seems to be following him.

Photo 120 was taken during a circus and shows an orb with an elephant and it almost appears as if the elephant is using the orb as a soccer ball. It also appears that the man has a set of wings. Is he an angel or is there one behind him? Photo 121 was taken by Monika Moehwald-Doelz and shows a flock of sheep and orbs.

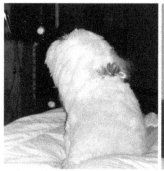

Photo 114 (left). Miss Mollie stares at orb. Photo 115 (right). Winnie watches zooming orb. © Virginia Hummel.

Photo 116 (left). Petie with an orb friend. Photo 117 (right). Winnie with an orb on her head ©Virginia Hummel.

Photo 118 (left). An owl with and orb. Photo 119 (right). A dog with a small orb above his head. © Larry White Buffalo.

PETS AND ORBS

Photo 120 © Toni Braun. An elephant and orb. Notice a pair of wings in the man. Is he an angel? Or is there one behind him?

Photo 121 © Monika Moehwald-Doelz. Orbs with a flock of sheep.

CHAPTER THIRTEEN

"There are two ways to be fooled; one is to believe what isn't true, the other is to refuse to believe what is true."

~ Soren Kierkegaard

Believing is Seeing

Paul Robb worked as an Optical Design and Systems Engineer at both Kodak and Lockheed, and spent thirty-nine years in the Aerospace Industry. He holds thirty-two patents, mostly in optical design and has forty-two publications in recognized technical journals on optical design, testing, and materials. He is the author of *The Kindness of God: How God Cares for Us.*[87]

In July of 2012, I sat down with Paul to discuss the subject of orbs and the optical issues that arise with cameras when photographing them. Paul appeared to be a diehard skeptic of orbs and he systematically countered each photo I showed him with an explanation of "diffraction point spread function"[88] or "splash back" from dust particles. Paul said:

> Diffraction Point Spread Function (PSF) (Photo 122) describes the response of an imaging system to a point source. In simple terms, if we poked a tiny hole through a piece of cardboard and shined a light through it, a camera on the other side, positioned a few feet away, would not

capture a pinpoint of light because as the light travels from the hole, it spreads out in light waves to produce a diffraction pattern of concentric rings of light surrounding a central, bright disk.

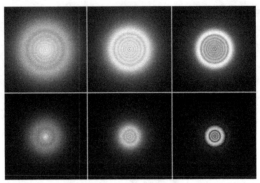

Photo 122 © Wikipedia. Diffraction point spread function.

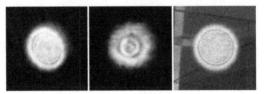

Photo 123 © Virginia Hummel. Orbs with PSF similarities.

After my meeting with Paul, I began to research Diffraction Point Spread Function (PSF). Similar concentric circles can be seen in orb photos (Photo 123) and I will have to admit they look similar to PSF. I had always wondered why some orb photos had them and other orb photos did not.

"Fresnel fringe" is another name for optical diffraction phenomena and resemble some orb photos. Is it possible that the combination of the light energy emitted from an orb, coupled with digital photography, creates images that are similar to these diffraction phenomena?

What also came to my attention were the differing descriptions of lights from near-death experiences. Some called them a "ball of light" and others referred to them as a "speck of light." I wondered if the balls of light and specks of light represented the same thing, but were merely captured differently on camera. Or were both the "speck of light" and "ball of light," in fact, completely different?

I have seen the balls of light or orbs, with my own eyes. I also see flashes of light or specks of light on a daily basis. The specks of light I see are similar to but different from "phosphenes," which are flashes of light (similar to "seeing stars") that are related to our vision. If I bend over and stand up quickly, I will see little bursts of lights called phosphenes.

These specks of light appear on or near my computer when I work on the book, for example. I also see them during the day in my bedroom where I spend the majority of my time working at my desk. I think I see them because I am aware of them. The instant they flash, my attention goes directly to orbs, but the skeptic in me also says "phosphenes." How do I know that what I am seeing is a spiritual phenomenon and not some random firing of cells in my eyes?

About a year after my meeting with Paul Robb, I was talking on the phone with Erica McKenzie and a large flash appeared in my bedroom between the dresser and the closet door. This is the same area where I photographed most of my orb photos. It is the location I filmed the *Sweetheart Orb* video posted on my website OrbWhisperer.com where a small orb responds to my request to move closer to the camera in order to film it for others to see. The large flash started as the usual speck of light I see, then shot toward me as a cone shape of approximately three inches in diameter, and returned to a speck before it disappeared.

Without a doubt, I knew this burst of light was not attributed to phosphenes. The cone shape that I saw with my eyes, *without the use of a photographic flash,* bore a similar pattern to the point spread function phenomena and was caused by something outside of the phosphenes of my own eyes—I am absolutely positive that it was something in the room that emitted its own light.

Furthermore, the color qualities of that light were somehow familiar to me in a spiritual sense. It was the most beautiful color of black I had ever seen. I saw white at the beginning, then purple, then a velvety black that seemed to encompass every color of the rainbow. The black reminded me of the peaceful velvety black I had experienced when I used the gift of divine light to intuitively read an elderly woman's state of health. She had not completely recovered from anesthesia after surgery. I have done this many times before with other people and received information about their physical and emotional health.

Divine Light

A few years ago, I attended a class on healing called "Light Therapy." As we sat quietly in meditation, our instructor guided us to imagine divine light coming in through the top of our heads and swirling down into our bodies. She then instructed us to visualize the divine light expanding out through our skin to create a brilliant egg of light around our body. She said the name of her client, someone we had never met, and said to imagine him standing in front of us where we would then lift this light over him to form a tent.

In my imaginary tent, I was to sit quietly in meditation with this "person" and wait for information to come to me. It could come as feelings, visions, emotions, sound, or even manifest physically. I almost laughed aloud. The skeptic inside me nearly jumped up and cried "baloney!" There was no way something like this was possible. How could I receive information through the ether from someone I had never met, who lived halfway around the world in New Zealand? It just didn't seem possible.

Since I had already experienced hundreds of connections with Spirit and I had seen orbs with my eyes, I decided it was best to keep an open mind and let the experience unfold. I knew that once I was able to experience something for myself, I could then determine whether or not it was real.

Once inside the tent of light, I waited. It didn't take long to receive information. Much to my surprise, I instantly felt physical pain in my body. My left knee throbbed so badly, I had to grab hold of it. This soon led to a deep ache in my left hip and ankle. Was I imagining this? Was I crazy, or was it really happening?

Suddenly my forearms and hands went numb. Now I knew I was nuts. I must have been dreaming this up; as if I were some sort of hypochondriac, just so I had something to share with the group once we began to relate our experiences…that is, if I dared mention this without sounding like an idiot.

My teacher finally told us to remove the tent of light and cut our connection with the man. She then had us draw in more divine light through the top of our heads, direct it into our hearts, and rev it up with love. Next, we were guided to shoot it out of the solar plexus in a fine stream of light toward that person.

As before, we accomplished it through intention and visualization, using our imagination. God, Source or I AM Presence would then direct the healing light to places in the man's body that needed healing. We were the vehicle. All we had to do was send it with the intention of helping him heal.

When we were finished, we took turns sharing our experiences. The teacher withheld all the information she had about her client until we had spoken. She would then validate if we were correct in our identification of the subject's physical and emotional issues.

Imagine my surprise when our teacher said the man had been in a devastating car accident and had a left knee replacement. He was constantly in pain and it affected his left hip and ankle. The woman next to me had also picked up his knee injury but not his hip or ankle. The teacher then mentioned that he was a recovering alcoholic. It affected his circulation and during the winter months as his forearms and hands would go numb. The man had other issues that people in my group had received that I did not.

Shaking my head, I thought, No way! How was this possible? How could I connect with someone in New Zealand when I was in Southern California? How could I connect with someone through my imagination and intention? I had never even met this man. Yet this is exactly what had just happened.

In Chapter Six, I mentioned Harry Hone and his NDE when he learned of his long-lost sister's whereabouts from a voice on the other side. During his near-death experience, he also learned that by using the power of visualization and imagination, we are able to bring into being that which we desire. He says, "All Power resides in imagination."[89] I desired to connect with the man in Australia and used my imagination and visualization to do so. It worked beautifully. I wondered if intention or desire was the key to connect with those on the other side.

Velvety Darkness

Over the next year, I continued to study with this woman and received my certification in Light Therapy. Using my intention, imagination and visualization, I had many opportunities to experience the same kind of connection with people I had never met and was able to pick up both emotional and physical issues. I have even pulled the light over a horse and correctly identified its problems. Although I can't explain exactly how this phenomenon operates, I do know that it was absolutely real and effective.

My teacher requested that another student and I visit a friend of hers whose mother just had surgery and was recovering in a rehabilitation clinic. Although she could sit slumped over in a wheel chair, her daughter reported that her mother was incoherent and "just wasn't there."

While visiting the daughter's home, my instructor, my friend and I went into a meditative state. I visualized divine light streaming into my body through my crown chakra located at the top of my head, and created a bubble of white light around me. Then I visualized pulling this bubble of light over the woman who was miles away in a rehabilitation center. I sat quietly with this bubble over both of us and waited for information to intuitively come to me.

The woman was someone whom I had never seen or met. All I had to do was sit still and wait to receive information. I immediately slipped into a blissful black velvety darkness. I was floating and no longer felt my body or the need to breathe. Surrounded by utter peace, I drifted in an infinite sea of tranquility.

Unaware of how much time passed, I could hear my instructor in the distance requesting us to wind it up and return to the present. Normally I would have adjusted and easily returned from my meditative state, but something was wrong. I couldn't bring myself back! My body was limp. I used every ounce of strength I had to whisper, "Help me!" I was aware that my instructor and friend moved near me on the sofa. They touched my arms and used their intention to pull me back from wherever I had gone.

Slowly, I drifted back from the velvety depths of that blissfully tranquil place and returned to the present. What disturbed me most about the experience was the realization that I didn't want to come back. This same blissful, velvety blackness was what I had seen in the cone-shaped speck of light while talking on the phone to Erica McKenzie.

Once I was alert, we discussed what we had seen when we each pulled the light over the woman. I told them that she was in a very peaceful place and would not return. I understood why. I too, did not want to return from that place. I told her daughter that she would die soon, and she did, just a few short weeks later.

Intuitively I felt a connection between the velvety blackness of the speck of light in my room and the infinitely tranquil darkness of my meditative state. The two were similar. It reminded me of a description Natalie Sudman mentioned in her near-death experience.

Natalie

Natalie Sudman, author of *The Application of Impossible Things: A Near-death Experience in Iraq,* suffered her NDE during a roadside bomb attack. She says during her NDE:

...It's as if darkness itself contains all light and has depth that can be sensed and seen...The stillness and vast space is profoundly peaceful in its silence...Imagine burrowing under thick down quilts in the most comfortable bed imaginable while a snowstorm rages outside.

Close your eyes then, and while you are feeling so physically cozy, enter into the limitless dark, peaceful, and creative space of the mind. Imagine the body as weightless and without boundaries within that, and the deep contentment that I felt in the Rest Environment might be approximated.[90]

I, too, felt weightless and without boundaries, drifting there in the velvety darkness where I had found the elderly woman. I wondered if Natalie and I were describing the same place. More importantly, I felt the velvety darkness and the speck of light in my room were somehow connected. It made the presence of the speck of light even more real despite Paul Robb's explanation of orbs as Diffraction Point Spread Function.

Why was I able to clearly see the cone shape without a camera? What did it mean? Was the burst of light from the "speck" in my room something that would create the concentric circles of Point Spread Function if captured by a camera?

When I focus over the top housing of my camera, a few feet in front of me as the flash fires, I can see specks of light that I can identify later in the digital picture as orbs with concentric circles. These specks sometimes appear as glitter. They will be present in one shot and five seconds later, the next shot has none.

As I sat with Paul, I was frustrated by his response that my orbs were nothing more than PSF. Undaunted, I continued to show him photographs and then finally, the video of the *Sweetheart Orb* posted on my website.

This video documents an orb in my bedroom responding to my request to come closer to the camera. I refer to the orb as "sweetheart." A small white orb the size of a quarter with PSF characteristics comes

ORBS AND THE AFTERLIFE

toward the camera at my request. It reacts to the LED light of the Apple iPhone, turns blue and increases in size. The point spread function (PSF) characteristics of the concentric circles and fuzzy corona disappear as the orb turns a solid blue.

Paul

After viewing the video mentioned earlier in this chapter, Paul Robb said he had no explanation for it. When I mentioned how I came to see my first orb without the aid of a camera, Paul interrupted me and shared one of his own experiences. Paul says:

> Many years ago, I was troubled by a family dilemma and one evening began to pray about it. Suddenly, a sphere of light appeared. It was approximately three feet in circumference.
>
> While the color varied, it appeared light blue with currents of blue running through it. It contained six people and I wondered at the time why they would all cram themselves inside such an itty-bitty ball of light.
>
> Since it was slightly transparent, I could see through the surface of the sphere to count the people inside. I couldn't tell if they were male or female, but I watched in surprise as part of a human hand emerged from the orb. When I paid attention to it, the hand receded back inside.
>
> I then heard a voice. I believe my grandmother was the spokesperson and proceeded to advise me on a path I was considering and praying about. She said, "Your path has been determined to be X number of years in duration (exact number withheld by request). You will leave with a sudden massive heart attack that cannot be detected in advance, and cannot be prevented. Make your plans accordingly.

Dumbfounded, I stared at Paul as he finished his story. Here was a man whose profession precluded him from recognizing the photos in

161

front of him as anything other than dust and particle splash back or PSF, yet he had just dropped a bombshell of a story and in all seriousness expected me to believe it. If I hadn't had the experiences with orbs, I surely wouldn't have been prepared. A smile of pure delight spread across my face.

"Did it ever occur to you that what you saw was an orb?"

"No, this didn't occur to me," he shook his head. "But that's what it was," he added. "In fact, this is the third experience I've had with a sphere of light. The other two experiences are too deeply personal to share with you."

Paul's description of the large orb with people inside appears to be different from the specks of light that I occasionally see. Were they, in fact, two distinct phenomena, or were they both somehow connected to the human soul?

CHAPTER FOURTEEN

"Imagine yourself as a luminous being of energy and light, because in reality…you are."

~ John Holland

The Newton Connection

In human form, our Earth suit takes on many shapes, sizes and colors. Our differences seem vast, yet I've discovered that we all share something in common. Our spiritual suit takes on shapes and colors too. Other people have also discovered this.

Annie

Singer and songwriter, Annie Kagan, author of *The Afterlife of Billy Fingers: How My Bad-Boy Brother Proved to Me There's Life After Death*, tells the story of her deceased brother, Billy, who visits her and teaches her about the afterlife.[91] He sometimes appears as a blue-white light above her bed. Annie says:

> Ten days later, at dawn, I saw an oval-shaped blue light hovering high above my bed. I knew it was Billy. I focused on the light, and soon I could hear his voice, which had become even more languorous than before.[92] [At another time] I was able to see the blue ball of light Billy identified as Tex's brother floating in the corner of the room.'[93]

Billy also describes a giant blue white sphere of light on the other side that is similar to the descriptions of near-death experiencers. He says:

> All beings carry the light from this sphere in them. That's why philosophers say that we are one…The light from the sphere propels your soul into your body when you're in the womb. It then becomes the invisible force that gives you life.
>
> And when the time is right, this same light launches your soul right up into the healing chamber at the moment of your so-called death… Then, instead of carrying the light inside you, the light will carry you inside it.[94]

Many of us would love to believe that Annie's brother has given us a beautiful glimpse into the afterlife, hoping we are more than just a physical body, and that we do survive our so-called "death." Billy's description echoes Dr. Tony Cicoria's description in Chapter Seven when he said he felt himself become a "ball of bluish white light" after he left his body.

When pondering the meaning "instead of carrying the light inside you, the light will carry you inside it," we are left to our imaginations to conjure up an image of Heaven and to wonder about the truth of our eternal existence.

Orb Photo 124 (enlargement) was captured in my bedroom one night with a face inside it. Photo 125 is a partial enlargement. I have yet to discover the identity of this person, but after reading Billy's description of the giant blue white sphere, I was immediately inspired to use this photo for the story.

When I first began photographing orbs, I mainly captured white ones. Thrilled when I started to photograph colored orbs as well, I wondered if there was meaning behind the colored orbs. I carefully ruled out the possibility of lens flare, which creates colored circles, disks of light and "energy beings" when shooting into a light source.

Photo 124 (left). Enlargement of orb with face taken in my home. 125 (right). Cropped photo of orb with face. © Virginia Hummel.

As I searched the Internet, I discovered all sorts of answers to the question of colored orbs. They have been identified as angels, archangels and unicorns, ET's as well as a variety of saints and sages. These particular answers were not conclusive enough to warrant my belief that the colored orbs were, in fact, all these specific entities.

But after ruling out the so-called colored orbs cause by lens flare, there remained a vast number of legitimate orb photographs with colors, sometimes even a single colored one amidst a gathering of white ones. I turned to science for an answer and discovered that colors on the visible light spectrum correspond with a different wavelength on the electromagnetic spectrum. Light can be measured in frequencies from the infrared range to the ultraviolet range; from red, orange, yellow, green, blue, indigo and violet and beyond.

After considering this information, I then wondered if the color of an orb was connected to a vibratory level or frequency that perhaps indicated its spiritual development. I must admit at this point that if an attorney were arguing the following theories, he might be shouting, "Conjecture your Honor!" but since we are talking about spiritual investigations, I have to bring in evidence from a variety of non-material witnesses. I may have been thinking like a paranormal Sherlock Holmes, combining fragments of evidence with my own intuition and life experience, but there were always nagging issues that bothered me until I stumbled on some interesting clues.

The question of colored orbs plagued me for several years until Bill Guggenheim suggested I read Dr. Michael Newton's *Journey of Souls: Case Studies of Life Between Lives.*[95]

As mentioned previously when discussing Dr. Wayne Dyer and my comments about blue orbs, Dr. Michael Newton uncovered the mysteries of life after death through hypnotic regression. He and his associates have regressed over seven thousand clients. Under hypnosis, the clients began to describe their guides and teachers, what they do during their "lives between lives," and when they choose to reincarnate for soul growth. They also described their soul groups or clusters, and the colors of the souls in their different states of spiritual advancement.

During these journeys, the clients left their bodies after death and spent time alone in order to review and examine their accomplishments and mistakes during their last incarnation. When that process was completed, they returned to their soul group or cluster. Newton proceeded to question his regressed clients about the description of other souls within their group.

Each group has a teacher who helps the soul with its spiritual growth. Just as with teachers on Earth who have varying education levels, these teachers also had varying degrees of spiritual knowledge. The spiritual hierarchy was denoted by the color they radiated.

As they progress, they take on other colors. She describes three other "Watchers" in her group as two having a tinge of yellow, and the third "turning bluish." The more experience and knowledge they receive, the darker the color becomes. She says the "intensity of mental power increases with the darker phases of light."[96]

One of Newton's clients whose spiritual name is "Thece" is an advanced soul. Her group has nine souls. She describes herself as a "glowing fragment of sky blue light with a few flecks of gold." Thece is similar to a group leader but prefers to be called a "Watcher." Her role is to watch and assist other souls if they need help. She describes the younger souls in her group as "dirty snowballs."

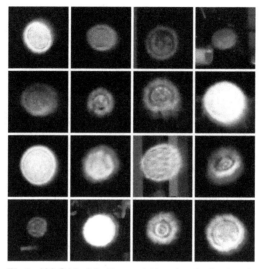

Photo 126 © Virginia Hummel. Un-retouched colored orbs.

Photo 126 is a collection of colored orbs, some of which seem to coincide with the descriptions of orbs throughout this book and are un-retouched. According to nearly one hundred case histories presented by Dr. Newton in his two books, his clients revealed that each color represents a step in spiritual development. White is the youngest or beginning stage of development. The darker the color, the more advanced the soul.

Newton states the various shades of yellow represent teacher or guide energy. Some religions refer to Guardian Angels, which Newton believes are actually our guides.[97] In his book, *Memories of the Afterlife: Lives Between Lives Stories of Transformation*, one of Newton's clients says, "There are five souls. They look like glowing yellow balls."[98] He also states that shades of blue represent Master Teacher energy while purple represents Ascended Masters.[99]

Photo 128 was taken in my home. There were numerous orbs in the original photo. Many of them were bright white. I noticed the colored orb on my fireplace and enlarged the photo. In Photo 127 I can see three-quarters of a man's face.

THE NEWTON CONNECTION

Photo 127 (left). Enlargement of an unretouched colored orb. Photo 128 (right). Cropped photo of the original orb. © Virginia Hummel.

Photo 129 was taken at a party. Notice the yellow orb with the concentric circles on this man's forehead. Could this be an example of a yellow "guide" or guardian that Newton refers to in his books? Could the purple orb in Photo 130 be an Ascended Master? There are also golden and white orbs in the photo. Could the blue orbs in Photo 131 represent Master Teachers? Dr. Newton says:

> I see the soul as intelligent light energy. This energy appears to function as vibrational waves similar to electromagnetic force but without the limitations of charged particles of matter...Like a fingerprint, each soul has a unique identity in its formation, composition and vibrational distribution.[100]

Alan

The following excerpt is from NDERF.org. Alan died one morning and rose out of his body. He says:

> ...becoming a small point of golden pure energy, I rose high above the Earth...I found myself in the presence of a being who appeared to me to be like a pulsating golden "ORB" similar to my state of being then, but much brighter and more energetic. At this time, I thought this being might be God. Later, I knew he was my Guardian Angel.[101]

168

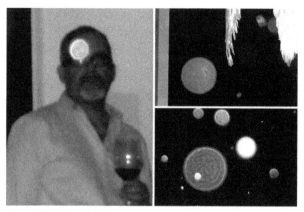

Photo 129 (left) © Virginia Hummel. Photo 130 (upper right.)
© Naomi Fugiwara. Photo 131 (lower right). © Monika Moehwald-Doelz.

Helen

In the book, *Testimony of Light: An Extraordinary Message of Life After Death,* author Helen Greaves channels Francis Banks. Francis says from the other side:

> No soul coming here from Earth's limitations, however advanced it may be in spiritual truth, is able to stand the stepped-up vibrations or the translucent Light of these High Planes…one has to earn every step of advancement.[102]

> Gradually I became aware of my fellows as "arrayed" in colors as in garments and by the depth or brightness or soberness or brilliance of their "surround" I came to know not only their characters, but their individual advance into the spiritual Realms.[103]

> We carry our own Light. The greater therefore the selflessness and illumination of our minds and the more positive our response to the higher frequency of vibration, the purer and brighter is the Light transmitted by us.

> Perhaps my greatest regret now is the realization that, while I was seeking and searching mentally, psychically and occultly to discover "the breakthrough" to Spirit for which I

longed, the Light of the Unity of all things, all creatures, all Beings, all Hosts, all Powers dwelt within me in ineffable glory. "I am the Light of the World," means just that."[104]

Helen doesn't specifically mention orbs in her book but she does mention groups of souls and refers to the colors of souls in relation to spiritual advancement like Dr. Michael Newton.

Henry W

Taken from NDERF.org, this NDE with Henry describes the souls as orbs gathered in cliques, which appears to validate Newton's client's descriptions of soul groups. He also describes orbs and their visits to Earth for the experience to learn. Henry says:

> The fact of the matter is that I died. I remember feeling my heart slow down until it stopped, at that moment my eyes closed. Not more than what seemed a second later I could see again. It was as if I had stepped through my eyelids...There behind me lay my body and at that moment I realized I had died...I became aware of others around me.

> There was no one I knew, but I sensed other beings. Soon I saw them as small golden orbs of light, each separate, an individual...I became aware of other voices, the orbs or other souls around me and I could hear them communicating with each other. There seemed to be cliques of orbs that were together. They spoke to one another about their lives on Earth and all they had perceived and felt. They shared not only in words, but shared the experience.

> If one orb couldn't understand, it disappeared and then reappeared. The orb somehow went back to Earth and experienced that "life" to further understand it. I understood that here time did not exist and these beings could manifest themselves at any time on Earth they desired.

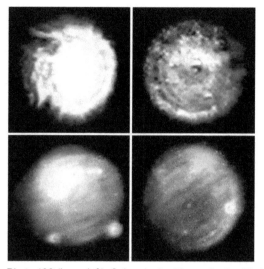

Photo 132 (lower left). Colored orb with small orbs. Photo 133 (upper Left). A face appears at the 10 o'clock position. Photo 134 (upper right). A face appears at the 1 o'clock position. Photo 135 (lower right). All © Naomi Fugiwara.

These orbs or rather "souls" would leave this realm and detach themselves with this universe and return to the universe of our Earth. There they would live and die, then return and share the experience with all the other souls. A soul that could not understand the experience could go and live that life also to experience that life. I learned we have many lives, past, present and future.

These souls, our souls, cannot experience certain things like pain, sorrow, hatred, and anger. Though these are negative things, it was important for them to understand and experience them. Perhaps to understand the motivations of human beings, or (and I believe this in my heart) to eventually evolve into a being like God - all knowing and understanding.[105]

After reading Henry's description of his NDE experience with orbs, my thoughts drifted back to my digital photos and the variety of colored orbs I had captured. Many people who have had a near-death experience often described themselves as "colored orbs." Skeptics would argue that the colored orbs in digital photos are lens flare and in many cases, they would be correct. However, it doesn't account for the remaining particle forms or embodiments. Could these remaining images be actual souls as described in NDEs?

Louis

The following is an excerpt from Louis Famoso's NDE, which happened during a car accident in October 1964 at the age of twenty-one. Louis writes:

> Instantly, I recognized a brilliant glowing ball of gold headed my way. It grew larger as it grew nearer and when it reached about the size of a beach ball, just above and in front of me it radiated brilliantly and transformed into an indescribable Being of pure Light, which now levitated right in front of me.

> It was larger than the tallest person I had ever seen, wider than two of me but so evenly proportioned as to be of Magnificent Stature. Its features were outlined as if made with a fine ink quill. Hair, face, and robe were all golden and flowing as would an electric charge perhaps even a nuclear charge. This was energy personified and as its form took on a more solid shape, all that was behind it did as well.

> It was as if the entire canvas of white I had come to at the end of the tunnel was now alive and I was part of it. Other figures appeared in front and behind the Being and myself. Soon there was activity all about, above and below, on every side, more beings, each of different brightness, sizes, and hues. Structures and landscapes sprung from everywhere all in a crystalline state, all inhabited by these lesser light beings—some winged, most not—some fully formed, others not—yet even others appeared only as glowing orbs of light and color, bouncing as would bubbles in a glass of carbonated water.

Just then, I saw five orbs of light. They seemed to be playing, swirling round and about the being and myself. They had appeared from the outlying landscape and I noticed they were all the same size and shape but of different hues as subtle as shades of rose petals, save one, which had a bluish hue. Two of the pinkish ones seemed exactly alike; the other two were yet deeper in shades of red and orange.

Before I could ask, *IT* spoke and said, "They, like all here are of you, who are of me, but these will come to you and you will care for them more. They will fly apart but come together at the time of the Gathering." I thought The Being might be telling me these were my children but I was only twenty-one, and not only had never been married, I had no plans to.

I didn't understand how all this was of me and me of HE when a magnificent crystal serving platter appeared and it shimmered the colors of many rainbows. In an instant, it shattered into thousands of pieces, each piece brilliant in its own right. Ever so slowly, now all the pieces began to rejoin themselves to, once again, form the original serving platter and I now knew what this Being of Light was showing me, we pieces are the platter. I was just one of those thousands of pieces, as were all those I was seeing here and those back in the "World."[106]

Eventually Louis had five children. Could the five colored balls of light that he saw in his NDE be the souls of his pre-born children?

Mischel

Mischel Thomas shared the following orb experience she had after the death of her soul mate Jeff. After a voice spoke to her from beyond, she describes seeing various colored orbs.

On my last day in Hawaii, something pulled me to the water. I love wading into the water in Hawaii as it usually is warm and womblike, however on that particular day, it was cold. I felt I needed to submerge myself, baptize myself and hopefully emerge with less sadness about Jeff not being here with me in his physical body.

Logically, I knew that he was in perfect place, more glorious then I could ever imagine, but I'm sure as you know, when the heart pulls at you, it pulls. And as a mere mortal, my heart was really hurting, and just so sad that as long as I was here on earth, we would never be able to even just hold hands together again.

I started to cry, but then a voice said, "Look up, move toward the west." When I did I saw one bright white orb, which made cry even more, but not out of sadness, out of joy. The sun was rising and there *he* was, a part of the sky and sun and all of it. I thought, oh my God, you are so amazing, Jeff, you get to be a part of it all. Then all of a sudden, the most miraculous thing happened. All around me, rising from the water, floating, hovering, were orbs, hundreds of them, in all sizes, shapes and colors.

There were three large violet, blue, red, orbs mixing together, forming this "organic" shape. I don't know if this makes any sense what so ever, but they almost looked like organisms in a petri dish, intermingling, dancing amongst each other. At this point, I knew I was having an experience like no other and said out loud, "There are spirits everywhere, I'm having a spiritual experience!"

I kept looking around and everywhere I looked the sky, water and land, there were orbs. At one point, I looked up and a plane flew over and three, large, translucent orbs were floating with it. I looked down on my black swim suit and tiny green, yellow and orange Orbs moved and pulsated together. The water at this point was no longer cold anymore, all was warm and womblike.

Brad

Brad Steiger is the author of one hundred sixty-eight books, with over seventeen million copies in print. His book, *One With The Light; Authentic Near-Death Experiences that Changed Lives and Revealed The Beyond,* describes a moment during his own NDE when he was eleven-years-old.[107] Brad fell off the tractor he was driving. Crushed and mangled beneath the tire and whirling blades, he left his body. Brad writes:

> The real me now seemed to be an orangish-colored ball that seemed intent only on moving toward a brilliant light.[108]

The following excerpt from *Life After Life*, by Dr. Raymond Moody, takes place in a hospital room and describes the soul in several different colors.

> I turned over and tried to get more comfortable, but just at that moment a light appeared in the corner of the room, just below the ceiling. It was a ball of light, almost like a globe, and it was not very large, I would say no more than twelve to fifteen inches in diameter, and as this light appeared, a feeling came over me...It was a feeling of complete and utter relaxation. I could see a hand reach down for me from the light, and the light said, "Come with me. I want to show you something."

> So immediately and without hesitation whatsoever, I reached up with my hand and grabbed onto the hand I saw. As I did, I had the feeling of being drawn up and leaving my body...I took on the same form as the light...It wasn't a body, just a wisp of smoke or vapor. It looked almost like clouds of cigarette smoke you can see when they are illuminated as they drift around a lamp.

> The form I took had colors, though. There was orange, yellow, and a color that was very distinct to me–I took it to

be an indigo, a bluish color. This spiritual form didn't have a shape like a body. It was more or less circular, but it had what I would call a hand...But when I wasn't using this hand, the spirit went back to the circular pattern.[109]

This story reminded me of Paul Robb's story where a hand also extended from an orb just before he heard his grandmother's voice. I have personally only taken three photos of an orange orb, one outside and two inside my house. I wondered if the orange orbs I captured were souls like Brad's soul, which he described when referring to the "orangish-colored ball" of light.

With the various eyewitness accounts of the description of a soul in a multitude of colors, we can now look to the visible light spectrum and science to validate the vibratory rate and development of a spiritual being manifesting as an orb.

CHAPTER FIFTEEN

"For those who believe, there are no words needed.
For those who do not believe, there are no words possible."

~ Saint Ignatius of Loyola

Faces in Orbs

They say a picture is worth a thousand words. How could one describe the following orb photos with faces inside them, without being able to actually see the photos? We begin to question the very fabric of our existence as fragile and imperfect human beings and ponder the larger questions of life after death, Heaven, immortality and the reality of the eternal soul.

A deeper message is at work here—one which seeks to illuminate our misconception of death and the illusion of fear it creates. Have you ever noticed the joy on a baby's face as she lights up with a smile? Nothing but pure divine light radiates from her very being. She is without fear. Every cell in her body vibrates in love, freshly tuned to God, Source and I AM Presence.

When we finally accept that consciousness survives outside the physical body, we realize this beautiful little infant came from somewhere besides her mother's womb. She came from a place of love, protected by God. It might explain why many of us are attracted to babies "like a moth to a flame." They are fresh from Source, unspoiled and unencumbered by the heavy cloak of our third dimensional fear, shame and criticism. We return to this loving, light-filled place when we finally drop our physical body.

I treasure every opportunity to bask in the innocence and light of my new granddaughter, Brooklyn. As I cradle her in my arms, I am at once my authentic self, with no expectations, wounds, fears or manipulations. She is connected directly to God, and I become love, pure, unconditional and limitless. It is a moment of deep truth, recognition of my spiritual self, and my connection to God and the Universe. I remember my home. I remember being loved for no other reason than just being me.

It is in this state of love with the complete absence of fear that I view the following orb photographs. Love is the vibration of God. Love does not die with the physical body but lives on eternally. The following orb photos offer us the opportunity to move past our limited beliefs and conditioning to prove what we know on a deep soul level: that we are truly eternal beings.

We are programmed to look outside ourselves to science and religion for answers; instead, we should turn inward for guidance. These photos are our link between Heaven and Earth. They are a way to derive comfort and connection to those who have crossed before us.

If nothing more, orbs are a fascinating example of the magic of Spirit in action. Dr. Eben Alexander, author of the New York Times Bestseller *Proof of Heaven: A Neurosurgeon's Near-death Experience and Journey into the Afterlife* says, "Orbs are one of the most readily accessible phenomena of the spiritual realm."[110]

Chris

While writing *Cracking the Grief Code*, a book about healing grief through orbs and other Spiritually Transformative Experiences (STEs), I realized that the best proof of the afterlife would be a book cover with my son inside an orb. So, I placed my order with spirit somehow believing that Christopher would give me an orb photo of himself at twenty-five, which was the age he died.

It never occurred to me that the orb photo I captured in my kitchen on October 27, 2011, shortly after I requested it, was Christopher at age six. The face of a young child appeared inside the orb but I didn't further pursue the identity. In fact, I created a different cover for the book, one without an orb photo of my son.

Over the years, I would come across the orb photo and wonder whose little boy he might be. In September 2016, I was completing *Orbs and the Afterlife* and came across a picture of Christopher at six years old. I immediately recognized the uncanny resemblance to the young boy inside the orb.

I enlarged and color contrasted the photo to discover the child in the orb was my son. Notice that the "v" part of his bangs above and to the right of his nose in the black and white photo matches the "v" part of his bangs in the orb photo exactly.

Photo 140 (left). Cropped original orb photo with face. Photo 141 (lower right). Enlargement and color contrasting of photo 140. Photo 142 (upper right). Christopher at six years old. © Virginia Hummel.

Imagine my surprise and delight to discover this after all these years. It is interesting to note that in the movie *"Heaven is for Real,"* Colton Burpo, the little boy who experienced an NDE in Heaven, tells his father that, "Everyone is young in Heaven."

Still, I wondered why would I receive an orb photo of Christopher as a child? Was spirit working behind the scenes as they did with the *Cracking the Grief Code* manuscript when they produced the orb photo of Chris as a child?

We know that the loss of a young child pulls at the heartstrings more so than the loss of an adult. I have to say that seeing Christopher as a child on the cover is far more emotional for me than had it been him as an adult. Could Spirit have a marketing plan?

I have learned in the past ten years to never underestimate the power of Spirit and God Almighty. There is a part of me that concedes that I have just been the channel through which Spirit delivered both *Cracking the Grief Code* and *Orbs and the Afterlife*. I am also most humbled by the experience.

Marcus

Marcus "Hoody" Lang from Sydney, Australia, shared an orb picture he took with a face inside it. In the original photo taken at night, the small orb appeared above a building. (Photo 135, lower right.) After zooming in on it, Marcus was surprised to discover a very detailed human face. He then enlarged and color contrasted the entire orb Photo 136 (lower left photo and inset square) and showed the picture to his wife. She was surprised to see the face of her deceased father Photo 137 (upper left) and is the color enhancement of the orb and face of Photo 135. Photo 138 (upper right) is a picture of Marcus's deceased father-in-law.

There is a mantra I repeat when I teach orb photography–*Don't assume until you zoom.* Marcus's enlarged photo delivers a dramatically clear human face captured inside an orb. This photograph appears to validate what many in the orb community think that these beautiful balls of light can be a manifestation of the soul or consciousness energy of a departed loved one.

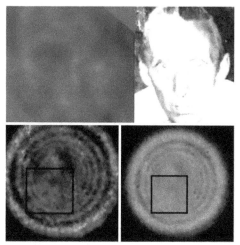

Photo 136 lower right). Original photo. Photo 137 (lower left). Color contrasted. Photo 138 (upper left). Enlargement. Photo139 (upper right). Marcus's father-in-law. All photos © Marcus Lang.

Linda

Linda Strausbaugh was kind enough to share Photo 143 with me. On December 26, 2012, Linda and her stepdaughter decided to go shopping. She says, "It was snowing pretty hard. On our way to the store, we noticed how beautiful this tree looked with the fresh new snow on it. I just happened to have my small Nikon CoolPix camera with me. After returning home I uploaded these and was quite surprised to find the face in the orb!"

Photo 143 (left) © Linda Strausbaugh. Orb with a face inside. Photo 144 (right) © Alethea Tucker. A face appears inside an orb captured at a battlefield.

Alethea

Alethea Tucker captured this photograph at an old battlefield site in South Carolina. Can you see the man's face inside the orb in Photo 144? It is a three-quarter profile. As a reader, you may or may not be able to see the faces. Some faces are extremely clear and others take a while to appear. It is much like the Magic Eye picture books with repeating patterns, which allow some people to see 3D images by focusing on 2D patterns. Once you begin to see the faces, they become more easily apparent in other orb photos.

Photo 145 (left). An orb appears after praying to Jesus. Photo 146 (right). Enlargement of orb in Photo 145. © Sue-ann Shay Meyer.

Sue-ann

Sometimes we are lucky enough to capture a photo of a spiritual experience. These photographs can be invaluable when trying to explain an event that many times can be life altering.

In May of 2004, Sue-ann Shaye Meyer had just finished a ten-day fast. (Photo 145) She had been praying to Jesus and felt a presence near her. Her husband decided to take a photo of her. She said, "I never saw the light next to me that night. My husband saw it."

He said, "Sue-ann, I cannot take a picture of you because there is a blinding light next to you."

"I only saw the bright circle on the picture, which I then took to the photo shop to enlarge and contrast for me. It was then that I saw the face inside the circle." (Photo 146) Some are more cartoon-like and others look like animals.

With practice, many people are beginning to see one if not many faces inside of orb photos. Although they may not be as photo ready and clear as these examples, the faces are nevertheless apparent. Some are more cartoon-like and others look like animals.

Photo 147 (left). A face appears inside of an orb captured at Humboldt Redwoods State Park.148 (right). Enlargement. Both photos © Aaron.

Aaron

Photo 147 came from a man named Aaron in 2013. Aaron said he had been hiking in Humboldt Redwoods State Park in Northern California. The photo was quite startling and my immediate thoughts were that this photo had been altered. *It can't be real.* After checking the photo metadata, I discovered that Aaron's photograph was an original photo taken January 1, 2002.

The face inside the orb looks to me to be a Native American. Because I have seen so many faces inside orbs, most notably the clarity of Marcus Lang's father-in-law, I have to concede that it is possible to capture very clear photos of faces inside of orbs. That said, however, my skeptical nature still looks for evidence to the contrary. I wish we had the ability to focus our cameras on these orbs instead of having to blindly capture these photos. I suspect then we would see large numbers of clear faces inside them.

The Angel

My angel statue has been the center of hundreds of orb photographs. It has been an active site for orbs and I have captured some beautiful photos with her surrounded by these beings. In the following Photos 155 and 156 (enlargement) a face appears inside an orb.

As I posted these in the book, I was forced to search through hundreds of files containing thousands of orb photos to find the originals. I came across another angel orb photo and discovered a second orb with the same face inside of it. They were taken two days apart. The following two photos are a side by side comparison of Photo 157 and Photo 156.

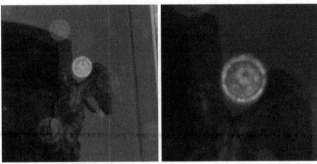

Photo 155 (left), Photo 156 (right) Enlargement © Virginia Hummel. A face appears inside an orb.

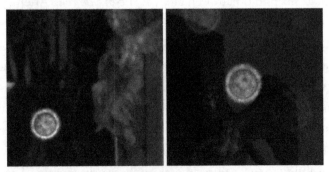

Photo 157 (left), Photo 156 (right) © Virginia Hummel. Two orbs with the same face.

The face inside appears to be the same, yet I do not recognize who it is. I have seen hundreds of orbs photos with faces, even animal faces, but the problem remains trying to enlarge these photos without distortion so that others may also be able to see them.

We have no way as of yet to focus on an orb because they are generally invisible to the naked eye, which means we have no definitive way to capture consistently clear orb photos. It is a random process. Orb photos have also been taken with multiple faces inside them but the quality is generally degraded as we try to highlight the faces and enlarge the photo.

Orbs and Consciousness

Can we really connect with those who have crossed over? Are our loved ones nearby? Are we watched over and aided by the spirit realm? If so, is it possible to ask them to appear as an orb?

Some people may feel that they aren't able to have a spiritual experience, while others have multiple or ongoing after-death communication with their loved ones. The digital camera offers the opportunity for everyone to experience the most readily accessible phenomena of the spiritual realm: the orb phenomenon.

When we capture orb photos and specifically photos where we ask our loved ones to participate, we have no longer classified ourselves as unable to have a spiritual experience; instead, we have stepped forward and participated in life on a multidimensional level.

We have stepped forward boldly in the knowledge that we are more than just our physical bodies. We have taken the leap of faith, produced results and realized that if we choose to, we can have all kinds of spiritual experiences. The door to endless possibilities is opened wide when we discover we no longer need to be a self-limiting but can, instead, be capable of anything through the power of Source.

Carol— Orbs Often Reveal Hidden Stories

Carol Danforth, a neonatal intensive care nurse in Southern California, has shared some of her wonderful orb photos and stories with me. The following true story is an example of someone willing to make the leap and produce results. She sent me Photo 153 without an explanation and asked for my opinion. After enlarging it, I could see a man's face in the orb. He is facing three-quarters to the right, but something was amiss. I could see his left eye, (Photo 154), but not his right one. Something was wrong with it. I emailed Carol and mentioned the man I saw in the orb, but I felt silly about mentioning the man's eye. I didn't trust the information I had received. She replied with the following story the next day.

Carol was at a gathering with her friend Nancy Myers to teach their first orb photography class. A couple who attended the class that evening had asked her brother-in-law to appear very bright in the photo so she couldn't miss him. Carol says:

Photo 153 (left), A woman asked her deceased brother-in-law to appear as a bright orb. Photo 154 (right). Enlargement. © Carol Danforth.

Thirty-some-odd years ago, when Gina and her husband were dating, she set up a blind date at the movies for her husband's brother. I guess he had something wrong with one of his eyes and was so self-conscious about it he wouldn't talk to girls, let alone date.

Well, he was really resistant and did not want to meet them at the theater. Gina begged, cajoled and finally talked him into coming. Wouldn't you know the girl didn't show up! He was understandably upset and he did not want to stay for the show that evening.

186

He left and, sadly was killed in a car accident on the way home. Gina has been feeling responsible for his death ever since. When she was standing there for the picture below she asked her brother-in-law to be there and she asked him to be "very bright" so she couldn't miss him. This is the picture that I took. She asked me if I thought it was her brother-in-law. I said yes.

I mentioned my concern about his right eye to Carol and asked her to ask Gina which one was injured. She validated it was his right eye, the one obscured in the photo. I also told Carol of an intuitive hit I received from the photo that her brother-in-law had actually taken his own life on the drive home.

Carol spoke with Gina and confirmed that she had also suspected this. Since his death, Gina had been hoping to connect with her brother-in-law. This orb photo taken by Carol Danforth helped to alleviate the pain and guilt Gina had carried all these years.

Many times, it is easy to detect the faces inside the orbs with the zoom of your camera after capturing an orb photo. Enlarging them and trying to print these photos are difficult at best because the picture degrades. Print on demand books lack the quality control needed to ensure clear photos. If you are having trouble seeing some of these faces due to print quality, please visit OrbWhisperer.com.

Knock Knock

Those willing to take a leap of faith are discovering they are able to communicate with orbs through thought and verbal requests. Many of the people I know who take orb photos on a regular basis are discovering they are able to interact with the consciousness associated with their departed loved one, who then appear in the form of an orb. During the past three years, I have had many distractions while writing this book. I have needed to be present for my family off and on during which time I was unable to write. My initial response was frustration but I noticed that the times I was forced to step away from the book I always returned to it with another new story, photo or bit of information essential to the message in the book.

An interesting thing I noticed was the feeling of being helped along by Spirit. As I sat at a table in the midst of writing this book, I felt a strong presence on my left and the overwhelming urge to grab my camera. Photo 149 is the orb I captured on my first shot. I distinctly felt the presence of someone. The identity is still unknown to me but I sensed that it was a male. I have also sensed someone nearby assisting me as I write. The presence may be one in the same.

Someone asked me if that particular orb had been present at other times. I wondered, and then began a search through five years of digital orb photos. It was a daunting task to say the least. Spirit communicates with me through feelings. Photos 150 and 151 gave me the same intuitive feeling that I got when I viewed the one taken while writing my book. I wish that I knew the name of this individual and a bit about them.

Photo 149 (left). Orb captured on camera just after feeling a strong presence to my left. Photo 150 (middle), Photo 151 (right). Orbs which I believe are the same orb as I physically get the same intuitive feeling from them.

What I do know is that I have been helped every step of the way in this process. My intuition tells me that this particular orb and the soul attached to it have played an instrumental role in the creation of this book. I have stepped away for weeks at a time only to return and review my work with the distinct feeling that certain parts were channeled.

There was a presence I could sense in my bedroom where I spend a lot of time writing. In the past year, an interesting thing began to happen. I would hear a knock at different times of the day. It was so noticeable that I began to ask whoever it was for more clarity. *Did the knock mean I was on the right track? Did it mean delete the paragraph? Was I crazy reading something into the knock when it really was just my imagination?*

When I heard the knock, I thought of Spirit and the presence that has kept me company for the past three years. I have never felt uneasy or fearful; instead, I knew how hard Spirit was working to help me. In fact, at a lecture I gave in 2013, a woman approached me and said, "I am able to see Spirit and I wanted to let you know that when you were speaking there was a whole team of people standing behind you cheering you on and busily working away like you might see at an election office." She confirmed what I felt as I shared this message through the process of writing and speaking.

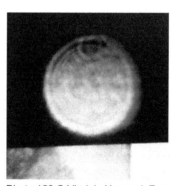

Photo 152 © Virginia Hummel. Face appearing inside an orb when asked who was present in my room.

One night in October of 2013, I climbed into bed and realized that I hadn't heard the knock in over a week. The moment it crossed my mind I heard it once again. My camera was on the bedside table. I will admit the thought of actually capturing the presence on camera was a little unsettling, but my curiosity to discover who was helping me was stronger than any fear I might have. I was going to share this message with the world, I would have to "man up" as my youngest daughter says and take the darn photo.

I said, "I heard the knock and acknowledge your presence. I would love to know who you are, your name, or anything you would like to share." I snapped a picture of an orb and inside I clearly saw a face.

The man appears bald and looks as if he is wearing glasses with opaque lenses. I can see also a mustache and a long straight nose. (Photo 152) I captured this orb in almost the same place (against my TV screen) that I captured the bluish orb with a face in Chapter Fourteen: The Newton Connection.

At this time, I still don't know who he is or his name, but I now have a photo of who has been nearby assisting me. Since then I have kept an eye out for a photo on the internet that just may lead to the identity of the man in the orb photo.

Although clear and detailed photos of faces in orbs are less common, we do find that many orb photos have faces that are more abstract. Some people are able to spot the faces easily and others are not. One doesn't need a face in the orb to validate the presence of a loved one, friend or helper. Just the mere appearance of an orb at a meaningful time can be enough validation.

Although orbs are the most prevalent spiritual phenomenon in digital photos, within the last few years another type of anomaly has begun to appear while photographing orbs. This new phenomenon produces just as many questions.

Skeptics are quick to say, "Photoshop" or "camera malfunction," but when the photographers themselves begin to experience strange physical effects while capturing the photos we realize these photographs are far more than a manipulated digital special effect.

CHAPTER SIXTEEN

*"If I tell you of earthly things and you do not believe,
How will you believe if I tell you of heavenly ones?"*

~ Jesus (John 3:12)

Highway to Heaven

Many of those who have experienced near-death have described a tunnel through which they pass in order to reach "Heaven." Until recently, we've been left to our imaginations to conjure up an image of this strange phenomenon. Is the tunnel real or a brain-based hallucination, created during the extreme stress of impending death?

Jack

Jack Williams and I met during a vision quest in the 1990s in the Four Corners area of Southern Utah. Jack is a professional photographer who lives in Ketchum, Idaho, where I lived at the time. Jack is a kindly older gentleman with a gray beard and a sparkle in his eye. During the holiday season, he becomes a perfect Santa Claus.

After our return from the vision quest, Jack showed me an unusual photograph he'd taken a few years earlier with a traditional 35 mm film camera. At the end of a West Coast photo shoot, he had gone hiking on the western slopes of the Sierra Nevada mountain range. He and his father used to hike this area and Jack wanted to find a suitable spot to spread his father's ashes.

Leaning his father's walking stick against a large boulder, Jack proceeded to scatter his ashes. Then he picked up his camera to commemorate the event. It was a profound and emotional moment saying goodbye to his dad.

He took three pictures in succession, one straight forward, one slightly upward and the third straight ahead. When he returned home, he developed the nearly two thousand photos from his trip. Jack noticed that one particular photo taken during his hike to spread his father's ashes was "out of focus," while the preceding and succeeding shots were normal. (Photo 158) Some of the trees were straight, but the rest began to blend and bend into a swirling phenomenon, completely distorted by a twisting effect.

Jack carefully examined the photo. What had caused the unusual twisting motion of the shot? Had he inadvertently moved the camera? Had he focused incorrectly? He was a professional. Out of two thousand shots during his two-week trip, this was the only one with such an anomaly.

Eventually he chalked it up to human error and tossed it in the trashcan. Then something nagged him about the photo. Recovering it from the trash, he tucked it safely away. He couldn't quite explain the swirling effect or how the tree in the middle remained vertical while the rest of the photo appeared to spin.

Over the years, Jack showed his photo to different people. Some thought there might be something spiritual or mystical about it; others chalked it up to human error. He enlarged the three successive shots and framed them. It certainly was a conversation starter when guests arrived in his home.

He showed me the photo in the early 1990s and recounted the story of his father's ashes. I was intrigued and intuitively knew this photo was significant. Although I knew there was a link between this photo and his father, I hadn't started my grief journey or the research that would eventually help me to make the important connection.

Around the same time I initially met Jack, a friend of mine told me a story that happened just after the birth of his daughter. He was lying on his bed with his sleeping newborn when the ceiling above him began to swirl. He said it looked like a vortex and as he watched, something came down through the vortex and entered his daughter's body. He wondered if it could have been her soul that he had seen descend into the baby.

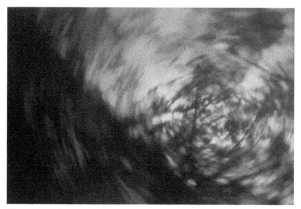

Photo 158 © Jack Williams. A vortex on 35mm color film.

Jack's picture came to mind and I wondered if Jack could have captured the moment when his father's spirit transitioned to Heaven through the same kind of swirling vortex my friend had described.

My friend's story coupled with Jack Williams's photo firmly embedded themselves in my consciousness. They lingered there for more than two decades, patiently waiting for the moment I would realize their significance to my own grief journey and research.

Every now and then, over the next twenty years, I thought about Jack's photograph. Then one day in the spring of 2012, I called Jack to talk about my work and my theory about his photograph. It had been nearly twenty years since we'd spoken. Jack was delighted to hear from me. I told him I believed he had captured a photograph of a vortex and the tunnel that we may pass through during our transition from this life to the afterlife. It certainly made sense, since he took it directly after he had scattered his father's ashes.

I asked if he would consider sharing the photo with me. He said for the past six months he had also been thinking about the photo. How odd that after twenty some years we both had a sudden renewed interest in that photograph. Were we sensing the same urgency to share it with the world? He was happy to let me use it.

During my research, I learned that in the late 1950s Nikolai Kozyrev discovered what the Russians call "torsion." Russian scientists believe that torsion is produced by the interactions between elementary particle spins, which generate a twisting of space. Russian researchers have published numerous experiments to prove that this torsion energy is the same as subtle energy.

According to Claude Swanson, Ph.D., author Life Force, the Scientific Basis: *Volume 2 of the Synchronized Universe:*

> Forms of this [subtle] energy appear to decrease entropy, slow down the flow of time, and promote order within a system…Just as torsion or subtle energy affects light; it also affects virtually every other force known to physics…subtle energy affects gravity, mass, time and many other physical properties, subtle energy also interacts with consciousness.[111]

Míceál

As mentioned previously, in 2010 my research on orbs led me to *The Orb Project.*[112] Co-author Míceál Ledwith had captured several pictures similar to Jack's photograph, but his photos contained orbs along with the swirling vortex. Míceál says, "I have photographed what I believe to be conditions that led to a full-fledged torsion vortex."[113]

Míceál had been taking photographs outside with his camera mounted on a tripod when he noticed the camera began to refocus itself. Although he couldn't immediately see anything unusual in its path, the camera certainly could. In or up against the tree line, he noticed with his bare eyes a large round object similar to an orb. It was approximately twenty to thirty feet high with a corresponding width. He says, "Directly after I detected this large object I had four or five photographs in a row that were out of focus or distorted in some way."[114] A few nights later, Míceál captured an astonishing example of a torsion vortex. Measuring with his hands, he estimates the grey energy sphere to be two and a half to three feet in diameter. (Photo 159).

Notice in the photo that the picket fence (lower right) is still vertical in the background as is Míceál. We see a tunnel forming with orbs in various states of manifestation. We can also see the twisting of space as it draws us into the vortex. The presence of orbs in different states of manifestation appears to be linked in some way to the presence of the vortex.

Could the orbs possibly use vortices to travel between Heaven and Earth? Míceál Ledwith says, "It is the gateway between the dimensions as I explained in my DVD, *Orbs: Clues to a More Exciting Universe.*"[115]

Photo 124 *Celestial Rose* by artist Gustave Doré[116] is eerily similar to Ledwith's photo. The original black-and-white engraving was created in 1868 for Dante Aligheri's *Divine Comedy* in which he uses his imaginative vision to describe the afterlife. Dante is shown the dwelling place of God which appears in the form of an enormous rose which houses the souls of the faithful.

Gustave Doré's engraving of the angels in the swirling tunnel is strikingly similar to the phenomenon that Míceál Ledwith has digitally captured with orbs emerging in and out of his torsion vortex. Some of the orbs in the vortex of the Ledwith photo appear to have a wing-like similarity to the angel wings in *Celestial Rose.*

Gustave Doré's *Celestial Rose* illustrate the same twisting of space discovered by Russian astrophysicist Nikolai Kozyrev and captured by Jack Williams and Míceál Ledwith.

Photo 159 (left) © Míċeál Ledwith. Used with permission. Vortex and orbs captured at night with a digital camera. Photo 160 (right) © Costa/Leemage /Bridgeman Images. Gustave Doré's "Celestial Rose."

Mya

As I sat at my computer writing this section, I decided what I really needed to firmly validate that both Míċeál's and Jack's photos weren't human error was a clear, color digital photo of a torsion vortex taken during the day. Thus far, my research had not yet produced that collaborative photo, so I looked toward Heaven and placed my order with God. The following day as I opened my Facebook page, there it was. (Photo 161)

I was stunned at how quickly Spirit works in regards to the information requested to complete this book. Now I had a beautiful clear, perfect, color example for the book. Photographer Mya Gleny had no idea what she had captured, but she was kind enough to allow me the privilege of using it. This is an incredible example of almost instant manifestation. It is uncanny how quickly the force of Spirit works whenever I've asked for help with this book.

Both Jack's and Míċeál's vortex photos appear to demonstrate the same anomalous effect as Mya Gleny's photo[117] although Jack's was taken with a traditional 35mm camera. If I hadn't seen Jack's photo taken twenty-five years ago, I may have questioned the authenticity of Mya's photo.

196

Photo 161 © Mya Gleny. A vortex taken with a digital camera.

Photo 162 © Diana Davatgar. Vortex forming in tree with orbs.

My sources swear they did not tamper with their photos in any way. Furthermore, Mya says that when she takes shots like these, "I often feel like the world is spinning."

Diana

Diana Davatgar captured Photo 162 in the forest. It shows a vortex forming with an orb to right. There are a few other orbs in the photo. Notice that the rest of the trees and branches appear undisturbed. As with all unexplainable phenomena, we have differing opinions. Skeptics are the first to point out two things: 1) the photo is a digital camera malfunction, and 2) it was created using Photoshop or a similar program. Are they right or are these real photos of vortices?

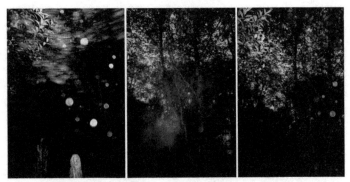

Photo 163 (left). A vortex with orbs. Photo 164 (middle). Plasma with orbs. Photo 165 (right). Slight plasma with orbs. © Gretchen Hermey.

Gretchen

Gretchen Hermey of Washington State took the following three photos in October 2012 with a Canon Power Shot 16 megapixel camera with 5x zoom. Not only does it show what appears to be a torsion vortex; it also contains orbs.

Notice in Photo 163 that some of the leaves and branches are in focus and others are out of focus; the vortex appears to be moving through the trees. The few orbs in the vortex remain in their spherical shape despite the distortion from the vortex.

Photo 164 shows a few orbs with a mist or plasma cloud mentioned in Chapter Two. Photo 165 shows more orbs and a trace of mist or plasmoid cloud. Míceál Ledwith says "Orbs occasionally manifest themselves out of the orb shape into plasma-like clouds."[118]

Plasma has been photographed with orbs and torsion vortices. Were these two women imagining this phenomenon? Was it a camera malfunction? Or could Mya and Gretchen have captured a torsion vortex?

Skeptics may insist that these photos are nothing but camera malfunctions or trick photography, yet author Míceál Ledwith was actually able to see an orb-like object near the trees approximately twenty to thirty feet high and wide when he captured a vortex with his digital camera.

Photo 166 © Gretchen Hermey. Vortex with orbs.

Ellyn

Ellyn Hanson captured Photo 167 in August of 2015 while walking with her granddaughter near "Heart Tree" named for the heart shaped rocks left at its base. She had just taken her granddaughter to the Prayer Bell at the Botanical Gardens and walked the labyrinth at the hospital where they talked of meditation and her son, Morgan, who had passed away. Photo 166 was taken with a Note 3 smart phone yet the preceding and succeeding photos were normal.

Once again, notice the swirling affect and that the anomaly narrows in the center giving us a 3D perspective of a tunnel of some sort. I captured Photo 168 in November 26, 2014 while babysitting my grandchildren. It appears to be similar to the other vortex photographs. I hadn't felt anything unusual and only noticed it when I scrolled back through the photos I had taken with my Nikon Coolpix. The preceding and succeeding photos were normal.

Is it possible this vortex is linked to something spiritual in nature? Was her son Morgan with them on their walk?

We know that some people are able to physically see orbs, including children. However, if this vortex phenomenon is real, is it possible for a human to see a vortex without aid of a camera?

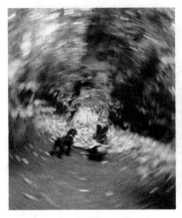

Photo 167 (left) © Ellyn Hanson. A vortex taken near Heart Tree. Photo 168 (right) © Virginia Hummel. A vortex captured inside the house.

Catriona

Australian born Catriona McKenzie is a writer and director of critically acclaimed and award winning short films, a multi-award winning documentary, a director of an Emmy nominated television series, and a director and screen writer of the new feature film, *Satellite Boy*.[119] In 1998, Catriona found herself face-to-face with a vortex while hiking in Ireland. She says:

It was a grey, drizzly afternoon in Glendaloch as I hiked through a lush green forest. I was exhausted and not really paying attention to where I was walking. Approximately five hundred meters (about a half mile) up the path, a tunnel or vortex appeared.

It was round and about twice my height and as wide as it was tall. It had depth to it like a whirlpool and was on the same plane as my body, but at a distance. The edges appeared blurred. I suddenly felt dizzy and nauseous.

In the film industry, we have a special effect called a "track zoom." To create the shot, the camera is moved away from the subject (along a dolly track), as the camera lens zooms in. It gives you a very disorienting feeling much like the vortex I encountered on my walk.

I had never seen anything like it and certainly hadn't a clue as to what it could be. Being one-quarter Aborigine, I am used to walking in the bush and seeing different things, but I knew I shouldn't be there. I immediately turned and walked the other way. I didn't understand it and I knew I didn't want to get caught up in it.

It wasn't until I saw the photos on the *Orb Whisperer* website and spoke to Virginia that I recognized and began to understand what I had seen so many years ago.

I wondered if the tunnel or vortex Catriona saw was similar to the photographs taken by Jack, Míċeál, Mya and Gretchen and Ellyn. Was it possibly the same type of phenomenon seen by my friend with his newborn? As I continued my research, I discovered that some people who have a near-death experience describe a tunnel they travel through to reach Heaven and the "feeling of being in a vortex or whirlwind?"[120]

Some near-death experiencers also mention "a sense of moving up, or through, a passageway or staircase or tunnel; going from a place of darkness to light, from a physical world to a transcendental realm."[121] In one account, a person who experienced near-death found himself in a clockwise spinning vortex.[122] Some will also describe the tunnel as "a change in the sense of time—slowing down, speeding up, or simply timelessness."[123] This seems similar to the description of subtle energy or torsion that appears to "decrease entropy or slow down the flow of time, affecting gravity, mass, and many other physical properties."[124]

Pam

Dr. Michael Sabom, a cardiologist and author of *Light and Death,* considers patient Pam Reynold's NDE to be one of the strongest cases of veridical—or verifiable anecdotal evidence for an afterlife.[125] During a rare brain operation where she was both clinically and brain dead, she was able to describe the unique surgical instruments and procedures used during her operation. Pam says of her NDE:

> It was like the *Wizard of Oz*—being taken up in a tornado vortex, only you're not spinning around like you've got vertigo. You are very focused and you have a place to go. The feeling was like going up in an elevator real fast. And there was a sensation, but it wasn't a bodily, physical sensation. It was like a tunnel, but it wasn't a tunnel.[126] At some point very early in the tunnel vortex I became aware of my grandmother calling me. But I didn't hear her call me with my ears ... It was a clearer hearing than with my ears. I trust that sense more than I trust my own ears.

Ned

Ned Dougherty, author of *Fast Lane to Heaven: Celestial Encounters that Changed My Life*,[127] writes of his near-death experience at the age of thirty-seven when he collapsed on the ground and watched a cylinder funneling upwards form in the sky.

> As a massive field of energy began to form in the sky directly in front of me, I heard a loud, grinding mechanical noise as the mass of energy shaped itself into a cylinder funneling upwards. It seemed as if the darkness of the sky turned into liquid as the mass of energy curled like an ocean wave and formed a perfect tunnel that stretched into the heavens.
>
> As I stared into the large and imposing tunnel of energy, a shimmering, luminescent-blue field of energy began to float down the tunnel toward me. As it rapidly approached, I watched the luminescent-blue field mass into a form and begin to materialize into an image of a human being. As the image composed itself, I found myself face-to-face with an old friend. His name was Dan McCampbell, but I had never expected to see him again. After all, he had been killed in Vietnam.[128]

Raymond

The foremost authority on near-death experience, Dr. Raymond Moody details a case study from *Life After Life* that describes a NDEr who also encountered a tunnel.

> There was a feeling of utter peace and quiet, no fear at all, and I found myself in a tunnel—a tunnel of concentric circles. Shortly after that, I saw a T.V. program called *The Time Tunnel*, where people go back in time through this spiraling tunnel. Well, that's the closest thing to it I can think of.[129]

Bridget

The following two excerpts come from Dr. Jeffery Long's website NDERF.org. After a devastating car accident, Bridget left her body and began flying upwards where she saw a vortex and orbs. She says:

> What I saw could be described as a vortex. There was a hole in the sky surrounded by clouds and lightning like plasma. Within the hole were stars, but not the stars we see outside our atmosphere at night rather, the center of the universe.

> Like a galaxy swirling around the most brilliant light one could imagine. It was what I perceive to be the source. Just outside the hole were light orbs going in and out of the hole, they were different brightnesses, colors, and shapes.[130]

Paul

Paul was also in an auto accident. He describes a swirling vortex and being cocooned in a sphere. Paul says:

> As I realized I was about to be killed, a sensation as of a swirling vortex began that enveloped my whole body, which then concentrated in my head and I exited my body through the top of my head. I literally flew out of the top of my head.

I found myself travelling in an upwards direction in total darkness but with a marvelously wonderful sense of well-being. I was cocooned in what I perceived to be a spherical form. My initial thought was, 'if this is being dead, I like it.'[131]

Ann

Ann Clerkin, who lives in London, captured multiple vortices with orbs in Photo 169. She says she has been seeing both orbs and energy without a camera. Many NDErs describe a being of light that meets them in the tunnel, takes them through the tunnel or meets them at the end of the tunnel. Could these light beings in some way be connected to the human spirit and the orbs we are capturing on camera and near these vortices?

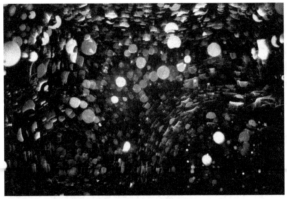

Photo 169 © Ann Clerkin. Multiple vortices and orbs.

Erica

Near-death experiencer, Erica McKenzie, BSN RN., was on a flight home from Orlando, Florida when she glanced out the widow of the airplane and witnessed what appeared to be a vortex and orbs. She describes the scene in her book, *Dying to Fit In*. Erica says:

Outside the window in the clouds a swirling pattern formed. It looked to be some sort of vortex. Bright balls of luminous light with tails moved clockwise in a circle like a miniature

Ferris wheel. There were too many to count. I had no idea what they were, yet there was something so familiar about them. Suddenly half of them stopped mid-motion and began to swirl counterclockwise.

Not one touched the other. The pattern seemed natural and effortless, yet I could feel there was some sort of propulsion to it. Strangely enough, I felt it calling to me. I mentally asked them to slow down just long enough so that I could study them. They heard my request and slowed so that I could take a closer look.

Suddenly, I realized what I was seeing. They were souls! They were the same kind of souls I saw in my NDE lifting off Earth and effortlessly flying into Heaven. They were the silvery, gold lights!

Each was a different size. There were souls the size of pencil erasers, golf balls, softballs, volleyballs, basketballs and beach balls and each of them had a tail. They were so ecstatic that I was able to see them and they began to communicate with me. I was downloaded with information along with a powerful all-encompassing love.

I realized I was with my Heavenly family. I was home again! As I continued to watch them, they would venture close to the airplane window and slow their vibrational energy just enough so I could see their faces. They were people! Tears spilled from my eyes. I knew them. I knew them all!

As they slowed enough for me to get a clear picture of their faces, I noticed their tails would fade. I don't know if they disappeared from existence or if they just faded to the point that I could no longer see them with my human eyes, but nonetheless, when they slowed to this point, I observed every detail in their faces. Each soul was contained in a perfect three-dimensional sphere. [132]

After reading these NDE accounts, it seems quite possible that these vortex photos with orbs represent the tunnel our soul passes through to reach Heaven after the death of our physical body.

We have read about:

1. Eyewitness accounts of an orb leaving the body at the time of death.
2. Near-death accounts that describe the soul as an orb.
3. Sighting of orbs following the death of a loved one.
4. Our ability to interact with orbs.
5. Eyewitness accounts of orbs appearing with one or more people inside them to impart information.
6. Eyewitness accounts of vortices appearing with orbs.
7. Eyewitness accounts of the twisting of space and tunnel NDErs describe they pass through to reach Heaven.

We have seen:

1. Photos of human faces inside orbs.
2. Photos of people interacting with orbs.
3. Photos of orbs appearing at meaningful places and times when requested.
4. Photos of vortices with orbs.
5. Photos that show orbs stretched and affected by this twisting phenomenon.

My research and experience lead me to believe that when we combine the evidence above, we not only see a compelling argument that the human soul exists outside the physical body and can manifest as an orb, we have also witnessed the "tunnel" through which we pass after the death of our physical body during our soul's journey into the afterlife.

Photos 170 © Diana Davatgar. Streaking orb in church.

CONCLUSION

The beautiful mystery of these luminous images can allow us to suspend our disbelief for a time, perhaps just long enough to consider the profound mysteries surrounding eternity and the afterlife. The stories and photos in this book have revealed what we all have the opportunity to experience when we open ourselves to the miraculous nature of Spirit.

Whether we recognize it or not, we are all connected to our Source—to the Creator, what we commonly call God. In *The Teachings of Don Juan: A Yaqui Way of Knowledge,* Carlos Castaneda said: "The entire truth is that the spirit reveals itself to everyone with the same intensity and consistency…"[133] It is up to us to align ourselves with that Source so that we too may experience healing from the beauty and grace of that Spirit.

The road to discovery was rough. In spite of the resistance I encountered from friends, family, acquaintances and peers, I followed an unusual path led by God, Spirit, and my son. In doing so, the joy remained and continued to burn out my pain. A large part of my grief journey involved my connection to Spirit, and with it came my connection to orbs. Orbs offered me a visual confirmation that something of a spiritual nature was happening around me. Often my camera could record what my physical eyes were unable to see.

Just as Jacques Cousteau's underwater camera revealed a completely new realm of life, my orb photography introduced me to another dimension of life. Orbs became an important tool in transforming my grief. They allowed me to imagine a world beyond my own and imagine that my son survived in one form or another. In the midst of my grief, I was lifted and filled with joy at their presence.

In the end, I chose to listen to my inner guidance and God. When human faces began to appear in the orbs themselves, it confirmed what my intuition had been telling me all along: that many of these curious lights appearing in our photographs can be a manifestation of our soul or consciousness energy. My research and experience with them shows me that *we are these beautiful light beings and we survive our physical death.*

When I introduced the orb phenomena to others who were also grieving, I discovered their experience was similar to mine. The presence of orbs provided relief, joy and comfort during a very challenging time of their life. Our connection with orbs created a crack for the light to pour in and it has helped many of us to shift our perception of death and transform our grief journey.

Orbs became the catalyst for my research and journey into the afterlife. Combined with the overwhelming information from near-death experiences, orbs became a tool to aid in my healing and to discover the eternal nature of our souls.

It is through the orb phenomenon and other Spiritually Transformative Experiences (STEs) that we can receive healing and validation that we survive death. We can use that knowledge and experience to help alleviate the pain caused by loss and the illusion of separation and begin to proactively comfort and heal ourselves.

Thanks to the digital camera, we now have a visual experience that possibly validates for the first time what mystics, spiritual leaders, and religious doctrines have expressed for millennia: that we are truly eternal beings.

We are not alone. In the midst of our darkest hour, love is all around us. As the veil thins between worlds, we are afforded the opportunity to connect with the magic and grace of Spirit. We've been given a window to the Divine.

ACKNOWLEDGEMENTS

I would like to extend my sincerest gratitude to God, Spirit, and all of the following people in their effort to help me bridge the gap between Heaven and Earth:

To my son, Christopher, who has worked diligently from the other side to open doors and assemble stories, photos and people to help move this message of comfort and hope forward. To my daughter, Olivia, thank you for your wisdom, patience, love and understanding, and my daughter, Kristin, for bravely sharing your journey with Spirit.

To Bill Guggenheim, thank you for your ongoing encouragement with this project. And thank you so much for your continued generosity and for purchasing the video cameras for me to film the orb phenomenon.

Thank you, Dr. Jeffery Long for graciously sharing some of the incredible NDE stories from your website NDERF.org.

I am eternally grateful to all the photographers whose generosity allowed me to share spectacular photos of this incredible phenomenon; especially Jack Williams, Míceál Ledwith, Monika Moehwald-Doelz, Naomi Fugiwara, Juan Carlos Ramirez Ibarra, Diana Davatgar, Mya Gleny, Gretchen Hermey, Gerry Werner, Marcus Lang, Nancy Myers, Patricia Alexander and Carol Danforth and Patrick Dalmollen.

I am also eternally grateful to all the brave, beautiful souls who stepped forward and shared their inspiring stories of loved ones, Spirit and orbs. As my dear friend Erica McKenzie says, "It is only when we come together that we can do great things."

Life *is* eternal. Imagine the possibilities!

Virginia

APPENDIX

Why Are Orbs here?

In answer to this question, I can only speak for myself, basing my conclusion on a combination of my intuition, research and experience. The consciousness contained in these brilliant balls of light described in the NDE and other spiritual experiences would like us to recognize that there is more to life than what we see and that life does not end with our physical death. I believe their hope is that we find comfort in this knowledge.

They want us to know that we are more than just a physical body. We are a brilliant being of light ever connected to our spiritual Source, and part of every living thing in all of creation. The presence of orbs should compel us to ask the larger questions and then search out our own answers to them.

My research and experience show me that we continue to live on after death and this knowledge allows us to experience life in a completely new way. I believe that many of these brilliant balls of light are a manifestation of the soul or consciousness energy of our friends, family and pets that have crossed over. I can imagine nothing more comforting after losing a loved one than to discover their essence or soul still exists and we can connect with them.

By taking photographs of orbs, perhaps we let them know that we are thinking of them too. Interacting with them gives us the opportunity to open ourselves to the beauty and grace of Spirit. It also allows us to shift our perception of death and offer those in grief a proactive way to begin their healing. What could be more comforting or serve as a greater testament to everlasting love?

How to Take Orb Photographs

What is the best technique for capturing a photo of an orb? Night shots are the easiest when you are just beginning because you have the contrast of a white or colored orb on a dark background. Make sure you have your flash on fill, your camera on auto focus and your battery fully charged. There's nothing more frustrating than running out of battery just when the orbs appear en masse.

Most people have the best luck taking pictures outside. Start with your backyard. I find I get great shots both inside and outside my house. As a novice orb photographer, be prepared to take at least fifty shots each session. Review them when you are finished and delete the ones you don't want. Be patient. Take ten in one direction then change your direction. Sometimes it is just a matter of aiming at the right spot and hundreds fill your frame.

As you get better at capturing orbs in pictures, you may only need a few shots each time to capture good images. Chances are you will be so captivated by them; your hobby will turn into a full time passion.

Remember:
1. Night shots are easiest.
2. Use a fill flash, auto focus and a fully charged battery.
3. Take at least five shots in the same direction.
4. Listen to your intuition.
5. The best shots may be behind you.
6. Zoom in to check for faces.
7. Review and delete unwanted pictures.

Trust your "Orb Radar"

Orb Radar is the feeling you get when "they" are around. I imagine it may be different for each person, but I just get a sense or a nudge to grab my camera. It happens when I either feel their presence from a change in temperature, feel Goosebumps, or when a thought that orbs are near pops into my head. Learning to trust your intuition is easy. Goosebumps usually confirm my intuition.

It just takes a bit of practice. Have you ever felt someone staring at you and you turn around and someone is there looking at you? You just confirmed what you were feeling. Have you thought of someone and the phone rings or you get a text message at that very moment from them? This is your intuition. It is a connection that we make on a vibrational level. Thoughts are things.

Once you have orbs on your mind, you have a great start at connecting with them. If you're not sure exactly what to do, take pictures anyway, and when you get some with orbs, just start tuning into that moment and the excitement that you feel. Soon you will feel that "excitement" before you take pictures and that will help draw them to you.

The angel picture in Chapter Four is the perfect example of "Orb Radar." I was not in the mood to take orb pictures, but the lamp on my bar started to flicker. I seriously tried to ignore it, but the message was just too strong. Spirit was trying to tell me something. In order to get the feeling to stop, I grabbed my camera and took a few shots. The Valentine's Day Orb was the result.

The "Orb Eye"

Once you learn how to recognize orbs, you will most likely begin to spot them in your old pictures. You now have the "orb eye." With practice, you can develop the ability to spot false orbs and lens flare from real orbs. For the serious orb enthusiasts, spotting the difference between orbs, dust, moisture, false orbs and lens flare is very important. Because we are so excited to "see" orbs in our shots, we can mistake dust, moisture or lens flare as orbs. *When in doubt, rule it out,* or ask an expert.

Don't assume until you zoom

Always zoom in on your photos before deleting. Great things come in small packages. Use your "orb eye" and carefully examine your photos. Today's digital cameras have very small viewing screens and you can easily miss a beautiful orb or a possible a face inside of it.

Lens Flare

Lens flare is the blight of orb photographers. Lens flare happens when you shoot into a light source such as the sun, moon, indoor or landscape lighting and windows or mirrors. I can't tell you the disappointment I feel when I see an amazing photo only to realize upon closer inspection that the "orb" or "energy being" is caused by lens flare. Lens flare can manifest as rings, circles, starbursts, discs or "energy beings."

They may be in a row across the image, but are typically spread widely across the scene. You can have both orbs and lens flare in the same photo. They can be a series of colored "orbs" or a mixture of discs, blocks, tapered cones and rainbow colors. The location can change with the camera's movement with relation to light sources. The shape of the aperture also affects the formation of anomalies in the photographs.

These photos are exciting and fun and stimulate our imagination, but they are not "orbs, vortexes or energy beings." They are lens flare. Experiment with your camera in the daytime and shoot into and near the sun. Tip and tilt the camera to create as much lens flare as possible. (Do not look directly at the sun with your eyes.)

Take pictures and discover the unique lens flare your camera creates. Learn how to spot the difference between real orbs and their energy and false orbs and lens flare. Moonlight, landscape and indoor lighting, and glass or mirror reflections can also create false orbs. Be vigilant when it comes to orb pictures. When in doubt, rule it out or ask an expert.

Types of Cameras

Different cameras take different orb pictures. I used a Nikon Coolpix for my photos in this book. The higher end SLRs can use optics or "hot mirrors" that block the infrared light emitted by orbs. Interestingly enough, we are learning that it is our intention that creates the ability to take orb photos. So technically, we should be able to get them with any camera. Some cameras just make it easier.

What I look for in a camera.

1. A good-sized viewing screen.
2. Touch screen zoom.
3. The shortest steps to delete pictures.
4. Shortest recovery time to next shot with flash.
5. Compact and easy to carry.
6. Opens and is ready to shoot quickly.

Orb Video

Cell phones can capture orb video and I have had great luck with my iPhone. It is important to turn the camera light to the ON position before shooting. Digital and Hi 8 video cameras can also be used with an infrared camera to capture orb video. It's fun to see orbs in motion, although a little patience and persistence is required to capture some great orb video. I have also used infrared lights along with an infrared video camera to capture orb video. Remember to set your intention to make a connection with this consciousness before you start, have fun and enjoy yourself.

Please visit OrbWhisperer.com to see some compelling orb video.

BIBLIOGRAPHY

Alexander, Eben. *Proof of Heaven: A Neurosurgeon's Near-death Experience and Journey into the Afterlife*. New York: Simon and Schuster, 2013.

Anderson, Joan Wester. *An Angel to Watch Over Me: True Stories of Children's Encounters with Angels*. New York: Ballantine Books, 2003

Assante, Julia. *The Last Frontier: Exploring the Afterlife and Transforming Our Fear of Death*. New World Library, 2012.

Atwater, P.M.H. *Beyond the Light: What Isn't Being Said About Near-death Experiences, From Visions of Heaven to Glimpses of Hell*. Transpersonal Publishing, 2009.

Atwater, P.M.H. *Near-Death Experiences, The Rest of the Story: What They Teach Us About Living and Dying and Our True Purpose*. Hampton Roads Publishing, January 9, 2009.

Castaneda, Carlos. *The Teachings of Don Juan: A Yaqui Way of Knowledge*. University of California Press, 2008.

Dougherty, Ned. *Fastlane to Heaven: Celestial Encounters that Changed my Life*. Hampton Roads, 2001.

Dyer, Wayne, Ph.D. *Wishes Fulfilled*. Hay House, Inc., Carlsbad, CA, 2012.

Famoso, Louis. www.loufamoso,tripod.com

Gleny, Mya. *Orbs: The Gift of Life*. CreateSpace (Amazon), 2012.

Greaves, Helen. *Testimony of Light: An Extraordinary Message of Life After Death*. New York: Tarcher/Penguin, 2009.

Grof, Stanislav. *The Adventure of Self Discovery: Dimensions of Consciousness and New Perspectives in Psychotherapy and Inner Exploration*. State University of New York Press, 1988.

Hall, Katie, Pickering, John. *Beyond Photography: Encounters with Orbs, Angels and Mysterious Light-Forms.* 6th Books, October 10, 2006.

Heinemann, Klaus and Heinemann, Gundi. *Orbs: Their Missions and Messages of Hope.* Carlsbad: Hay House, Inc. 2010.

Hone, Harry. *The Light at the End of the Tunnel.* American Biographical Center, June 1985.

Hummel, Virginia. *Miracle Messenger: Signs from Above, Love from Beyond.* Palm Desert: StarChild10 Publications, 2011.

Hummel, Virginia. *Cracking the Grief Code: The Healing Power of the Orb Phenomenon, After-Death Communications, Near-Death Experiences, Pre-Birth Contracts, Past Lives and Reincarnation.* Ketchum, ID: StarChild10 Publications, 2016

Kagan, Annie. *The Afterlife of Billy Fingers: How My Bad Boy Brother Proved to Me There's Life After Death.* Hampton Roads, 2013.

LaGrand, Louis. *Love Lives On: Learning from the Extraordinary Encounters of the Bereaved.* New York, Berkley Books, 2006.

Ledwith, Mícéál and Heinemann, Klaus. *The Orb Project.* New York: Simon & Schuster/Atria/Beyond Words, 2007.

Ledwith, Mícéál. *Orbs: Cues to a More Exciting Universe* (DVD)

McKenzie, Erica , *Dying to Fit In*, CreateSpace (Amazon.com), 2015.

Melchizedek, Drunvalo. *Serpent of Light: Beyond 2012.* New York: Red Wheel/Weiser 2008.

Megre, Vladimir. *The Ringing Cedars of Russia - Book 2.* Ringing Cedars Press, 2008.

Newton, Michael. *Destiny of Souls.* Llewellyn, 2005.

Newton, Michael. *Journey of Souls.* Llewellyn, 2010.

Our Ultimate Reality website:
http://www.ourultimatereality.com/vibration-a-fundamental-characteristic-of-energy.html

Puryear, Anne. *Stephen Lives: His life, Suicide and Afterlife.* New Paradigm Press, 1992.

Richelieu, Peter. *A Soul's Journey.* Ariel Press, 2011.

Sabom, Michael. *Light and Death.* Zondervan, 1998.

Shockey, Peter. *Reflections of Heaven: A Millennial Odyssey of Miracles, Angels, And Afterlife.* New York: Doubleday, 1999.

Steiger, Brad. *One with the Light: Authentic Near-Death Experiences that Changed Lives and Revealed the Beyond.* New York: Signet, 1995.

Strassman, Rick. *DMT: The Spirit Molecule: A Doctor's Revolutionary Research into the Biology of Near-Death and Mystical Experiences.* Park Street Press, 2000.

www.amazon.com/DMT-Molecule-Revolutionary-Near-Death-Experiences/dp/0892819278, pg. 123.

http://en.wikipedia.org/wiki/Dimethyltryptamine, pg. 24.

Sudman, Natalie. *The Application of Impossible Things.* Huntsville, Arkansas: Ozark Mountain Publishing, 2012

Swanson, Claude. *Life Force, The Scientific Basis: Breakthrough Physics of Energy Medicine, Healing, Chi and Quantum Consciousness.* Tucson, AZ: Poseidia Press, 2011.

Swanson, Claude. *The Synchronized Universe: New Science of the Paranormal.* Tucson, AZ: Poseidia Press, 2009.

Virtue, Doreen. *Archangels and Ascended Masters: A Guide to Working and Healing with Divinities and Deities.* Carlsbad: Hay House, Inc. 2004.

ENDNOTES

Chapter One

[1] http://www.imdb.com/title/tt0192937/

[2] Op. Cit.,78.

[3] Klaus and Gundi Heinemann, *Orbs: Their Mission and Messages of Hope* (Carlsbad: Hay House, Inc.2011), 118.

[4] Míċeál Ledwith, Klaus Heinemann, *The Orb Project* (New York : Atria, 2007), 128.

[5] http://www.orbwhisperer.com/Home_Page.php

Chapter Two

[6] Claude Swanson, *The Synchronized Universe Series: New Science of the Paranormal*, (Tucson: Poseidia Press, 2009).

[7] http://www.synchronizeduniverse.com/IntroductionVOLII.htm

[8] http://www.synchronizeduniverse.com/IntroductionVOLII.htm

[9] http://www.suzannegiesemann.com/#!more-on-suzanne/chcr

[10] http://www.suzannegiesemann.com/

[11] http://www.suzannegiesemann.com/#!about2/cv22

[12] Beyond Photography, op. cit., 148- 150.

[13] Míċeál Ledwith, Klaus Heinemann, *The Orb Project* (New York: Atria, 2007), 123.

[14] Míċeál Ledwith, Klaus Heinemann, *The Orb Project* (New York : Atria, 2007), 43, 44.

[15] Beyond Photography, op. cit., 165- 166.

[16] Vladimir Megre, *The Ringing Cedars of Russia* (Ringing Cedars Press, 2008).

[17] Ibid., 175.

[18] Ibid., 176.

[19] Megre, op. cit., 181.

Chapter Three

[20] Brad Steiger, *One With The Light* (Signet, 1994), 72.

[21] Míċeál Ledwith, Klaus Heinemann, *The Orb Project*, (New York: Atria, 2007).

[22] Anne Puryear, *Steven Lives: His Life, Suicide and Afterlife* (Scottsdale, AZ: New Paradigm Press, 1992).
[23] Ibid.

Chapter Four

[24] Klaus and Gundi Heinemann, *Orbs: Their Mission and Messages of Hope* (Carlsbad: Hay House, Inc. 2011), 7.
[25] http://www.brainyquote.com/quotes/quotes/j/josephcamp384345.html
[26] Klaus and Gundi Heinemann, *Orbs: Their Mission and Messages of Hope* (Hay House, Inc., Carlsbad, CA, 2011), 6.
[27] Patricia Alexander, Michael Burgos, *The Book of Comforts* (Templeton: Blue Epiphany, 2005).

Chapter Five

[28] The molecule DMT (N,N-Dimethyltryptamine) is a psychoactive chemical that causes intense visions and can induce its users to quickly enter a completely different "environment" that some have likened to an alien or parallel universe.
http://sprott.physics.wisc.edu/pickover/pc/dmt.html
[29] http://www.tokenrock.com/explain-third-eye-83.html
http://personaltao.com/taoism-library/shamanic-teachings/about-visions/what-is-the-third-eye/
[30] Ibid.
[31] http://balancechakra.com/?CategoryID=548&ArticleID=821
[32] http://www.tokenrock.com/explain-third-eye-83.html
[33] The pineal gland is a tiny organ in the center of the brain that played an important role in Descartes' philosophy. He regarded it as the principal seat of the soul and the place in which all our thoughts are formed.
http://plato.stanford.edu/entries/pineal-gland/
[34] http://johnsarkis.hubpages.com/hub/Descartes-Concept-of-The-Soul
[35] Op Cit. http://sprott.physics.wisc.edu/pickover/pc/dmt.html
[36] Rick Strassman, *DMT: The Spirit Molecule* (Park Street Press, 2001).
[37] Strassman, op. cit., 74.
[38] Ibid., 74.
[39] Ibid, 63-64.
[40] Ibid, 146.
[41] Virginia Hummel, *Miracle Messenger* (StarChild10 Publications. 2011).
[42] Virtue, Doreen, Archangels and Ascended Masters: A Guide to Working and Healing with Divinities c and Deities (Hay House, Inc., Carlsbad, CA. 2004).

[43] Ibid.

[44]Hummel, op. cit.

Chapter Six

[45] Max Velmans, *Goodbye to Reductionism, "*Toward a Science of Consciousness II: The Second Tucson Discussions and Debates" (A Bradford Book, 1998).

[46] Eben Alexander, *Proof of Heaven* (New York: Simon & Schuster, 2012).

[47] Ibid, 38-40.

[48] Ibid, 47.

[49] Ibid, 169.

[50] Strassman, op. cit.,76.

[51]Ibid, 146.

[52] Harry Hone, *A Light at the End of the Tunnel*, (American Biographical Center, 1985).

[53] Ibid., 23.

[54] Ibid., 27.

[55] Ibid., 141.

[56] P.M.H. Atwater*, Beyond the Light: What Isn't Being Said About Near Death Experience: From Visions of Heaven to Glimpses of Hell,* (Transpersonal Publishing: 2009).

Chapter Seven

[57] Raymond Moody, *Life After Life* (New York: MMB, INC 1975).

[58] Ibid., 36.

[59] Ibid., 40.

[60] Ibid., 40.

[61] Ibid., 40.

[62] Op. Cit., http://www.amazon.com/Beyond-Light-Experience-VisionsGlimpses/dp/1929661339/ref=sr_1_1?s=books&ie=UTF8&qid=1398028627&sr=1-1&keywords=beyond+the+light

[63] http://www.nderf.org/NDERF/NDE_Experiences/rachel_r_nde.htm

[64] http://www.synchronizeduniverse.com/IntroductionVOLII.htm

[65] http://www.synchronizeduniverse.com/IntroductionVOLII.htm

Chapter Eight

[66] Erica McKenzie, Virginia Hummel, *Dying to Fit In,* (CreateSpace, Amazon 2015).

[67] Maureen McGill, Nola Davis, *Live from the Other Side,* (Ozark Mountain Publishing, 2010).

[68] Claude Swanson, *Life Force, The Scientific Basis; Breakthrough Physics of Energy Medicine, Healing, Chi and Quantum Consciousness,* (Tucson: Poseidia Press, 2010), 263.

Chapter Nine

[69] http://www.amazon.com/Adventure-Self-Discovery-Consciousness-Psychotherapy-Transpersonal/dp/0887065414

[70] Peter Richelieu, *A Soul's Journey,* (Ariel Press, 2011).

[71] http://sharedcrossing.com/

[72] Louis LaGrand, Love lives On: Learning from the Extraordinary Encounters of the Bereaved, (Berkeley Book, New York, 2006), 189

[73] Wayne Dyer, Ph.D., is an internationally renowned author and speaker in the field of self-development. He's the author of over thirty books, has created many audio programs and videos, and has appeared on thousands of television and radio shows. His books, *Manifest Your Destiny, Wisdom of the Ages, There's a Spiritual Solution to Every Problem*, and the *New York Times* bestsellers *10 Secrets for Success and Inner Peace, The Power of Intention, Inspiration, Change Your Thoughts—Change Your Life, Excuses Begone*, and now *Wishes Fulfilled* have all been featured as National Public Television specials. http://www.drwaynedyer.com/

[74] Michael Newton, *Journey of Souls: Case Studies of Lives Between Lives,* (Woodbury; Llewellyn Publications, 2010).

Chapter Ten

[75] Joan Wester Anderson, *An Angel to Watch Over Me,* (New York : Ballentine Books, 1994), 6.

[76] Peter Shockey, *Reflections of Heaven,* (New York : Doubleday, 2007)

[77] Ibid.,126-133.

[78] Mya Gleny, *Orbs: The Gift of Light,* (CreateSpace, Amazon, 2012).

[79] Julia Assante, *The Last Frontier: Exploring the Afterlife*, Copyright 2012 by Julia Assante, PhD. Reprinted with permission from New World Library, Novato. http://www.newworldlibrary.com/.

[80] Ibid., 299-300.

Chapter Eleven

[81] Drunvalo Melchizedek, *The Ancient Secret of the Flower of Life, Volumes I & II, Serpent of Light: Beyond 2012*, (Light Technology Publishing 1999).

[82] Material excerpted from Drunvalo Melchizedek, *Serpent of Light: Beyond 2012* ©2008 by Drunvalo Melchizedek., with permission from Red Wheel/Weiser, LLC Newburyport, MA and San Francisco, CA, www.redwheelweiser.com., 26.

[83] http://www.meetup.com/foundation-for-mind-being-research-FMBR/

[84] Reiki is a Japanese technique for stress reduction and relaxation that also promotes healing. It is administered by "laying on hands" and is based on the idea that an unseen "life force energy" flows through us and is what causes us to be alive. http://www.reiki.org/faq/whatisreiki.html

[85] Klaus Heinemann, Gundi Heinemann, *Orbs; Their Mission and Messages of Hope,* (Carlsbad: Hay House, Inc. 2010) Photo 1

[86] https://www.youtube.com/watch?v=cDTlPXgqymo

Chapter Thirteen

[87] Paul Robb, *The Kindness of God: How He Cares for Us* (Denver : Outskirts Press, 2007).

[88] http://en.wikipedia.org/wiki/Point_spread_function

[89] http://www.amazon.com/Light-End-Tunnel-First-Person/dp/0960116842/ref=sr_1_2?s=books&ie=UTF8&qid=1398028324&sr=1-2&keywords=harry+hone

[90] Natalie Sudman, *Application of Impossible Things,* (Huntsville, Arkansas: Ozark Mountain Publishing, 2012), 58.

Chapter Fourteen

[91] Annie Kagan, *The Afterlife of Billy Fingers,* (Hampton Roads, 2013).

[92] Ibid.,79.

[93] Ibid., 129.

[94] Ibid., 94.

[95] Op. Cit., Newton, *Journey of Souls,* (Woodbury: Llewellyn, 1994).

[96] Ibid., 172-178.

[97] Michael Newton, Ph.D., *Journey of Souls,* (Woodbury: Llewellyn, 1994), 35.

[98] Michael Newton Ph.D., *Memories of the Afterlife: Lives between Lives, Stories of Transformation,* (Llewellyn, 2011), 91.

[99] Ibid., 112.

[100] Ibid.

[101] http://www.nderf.org/NDERF/NDE_Experiences/alan_mcd_nde.htm

[102] Ibid., 44.

[103] Ibid., 149.

[104] Ibid., 158-159.

[105]NDERF.org
http://www.nderf.org/NDERF/NDE_Experiences/henry_w_probable_nde.htm
[106] http://www.near-death.com/forum/nde/000/05.html
[107] Brad Steiger, *One With the Light: Authentic Near-Death Experiences that Changed Lives and Revealed the Beyond,* (New York: Signet, 1994).
[108] Ibid., 12.
[109] Raymond Moody, *Life After Life,* (New York : MMB, INC 1975), 69.

Chapter Fifteen

[110] http://www.ebenalexander.com/stories-of-the-eternal/key-resources/

Chapter Sixteen

[111] Claude Swanson, *Life Force; The Scientific Basis; Breakthrough Physics of Energy Medicine, Healing, Chi and Quantum Consciousness,* (Tucson: Poseidia Press, 2010), 143-145.
[112] Op. Cit., *The Orb Project.*
[113] Míceál Ledwith, Klaus Heinemann, *The Orb Project*, (New York : Atria, 2007), 56.
[114] Ibid., 57.
[115] http://www.amazon.com/ORBS-Clues-More-Exciting-Universe/dp/B001JHYA04/ref=sr_1_cc_1?s=aps&ie=UTF8&qid=1398185117&sr=1-1-catcorr&keywords=Clues+to+a+More+Exciting+Universe+-+dvd.
[116] Paradiso, Canto 31 : The saintly throng form a rose in the empyrean (Rose Celeste), illustration from 'The Divine Comedy' by Dante Alighieri, 1885 (digitally colored engraving), Doré, Gustave (1832-83) (after) / Private Collection / © Costa/Leemage / Bridgeman Images.
[117] http://www.myaglenywordsandpictures.com/
[118] Míceál Ledwith, *The Orb Project,* (Simon & Schuster 2007).
[119]http://www.imdb.com/name/nm1642908/
[120] http://www.eternea.org/NDE_definition.aspx
[121] Ibid.

[122] http://www.noetic.org/noetic/issue-twenty-three-june/physics-of-near-death-experiences/
[123] http://www.eternea.org/NDE_definition.aspx
[124] Claude Swanson, *Life Force, The Scientific Basis; Breakthrough Physics of Energy Medicine, Healing, Chi and Quantum Consciousness,* (Tucson: Poseidia Press, 2010), 143-145.

125 http://www.amazon.com/Light-Death-Michael-Sabom-ebook/dp/B004Q9T3FY/ref=sr_1_1?s=books&ie=UTF8&qid=1398182525&sr=1-1&keywords=light+and+death
126 http://www.near-death.com/experiences/evidence01.html.
127 http://www.amazon.com/Fast-Lane-Heaven-Life-After-Death-Journey-ebook/dp/B001QCWPPO/ref=sr_1_1?s=books&ie=UTF8&qid=1398184433&sr=1-1&keywords=fast+lane+to+heaven+by+ned+dougherty
128 Ibid.
129 Raymond Moody, *Life After Life,* (New York: MMB, INC 1975), 23.
130 http://www.nderf.org/NDERF/NDE_Experiences/bridget_f_nde.htm
131http://www.nderf.org/NDERF/NDE_Experiences/paul_o_nde.htm
132 Erica McKenzie and Virginia Hummel, *Dying to Fit In,* (CreateSpace, Amazon, 2015), 217-219.

Conclusion

133 http://www.amazon.com/The-Teachings-Don-Juan-Knowledge/dp/0671600419/ref=sr_1_1?ie=UTF8&qid=1398194266&sr=8-1&keywords=The+Teachings+of+Don+Juan%2C

About the Author

Virginia M. Hummel is a writer, speaker, and co-producer of an upcoming documentary on healing grief through Spiritually Transformative Experiences (STEs). Her deepest hope is to help guide others on a spiritual path to transmute pain, loss and grief into personal growth and empowerment.

She is a lifelong student of metaphysical, spiritual and after-death subjects. With the death of her youngest son, Christopher, she experienced a series of spontaneous spiritual events that helped transform her grief and find a place of balance and joy.

Virginia has been a researcher and experiencer of the orb phenomenon for over a decade. She is Chairman of Orb Encounters at **Eternea.org**, a publicly supported global non-profit research, educational and outreach organization co-created by Eben Alexander and John Audette. Eternea's mission is to advance research, education and applied programs concerning the physics of consciousness and the interactive relationship between consciousness and physical reality.

Please visit her at: **OrbWhisperer.com** dedicated to the orb phenomenon and **Virginiahummel.com** dedicated to healing grief through Spiritually Transformative Experiences (STEs).

Receive a **FREE Kindle** version of either:

Orbs and the Afterlife
or
Cracking the Grief Code: The Healing Power of the Orb Phenomenon, After-Death Communication, Near-Death Experience, Pre-Birth Contracts, Past Lives and Reincarnation.

Just Leave a Review on Amazon.com

then email me at **Virginia@theOrbWhisperer.com**

To see the clearer detailed photos from this book please visit my private page. **OrbWhisperer.com/book-photos**

Also by Virginia Hummel

  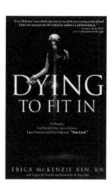

Cracking the Grief Code: *The Healing Power of the Orb Phenomenon, After-Death Communication, Near-Death Experience, Pre-Birth Contracts, Past Lives and Reincarnation*

Miracle Messenger:
Signs from Above, Love from Beyond

Dying To Fit In
Erica McKenzie with Virginia M. Hummel
Foreword by Dr. Rajiv Parti

(One woman's NDE with God)

Available at Amazon.com
Paperback
Kindle